LIVE

Like You
Mean It

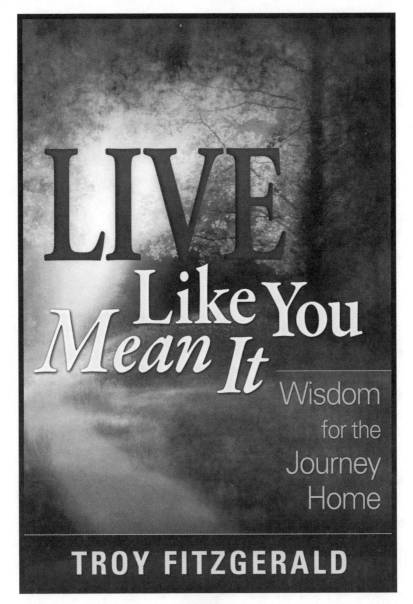

LIVE
Like You
Mean It

Wisdom
for the
Journey
Home

TROY FITZGERALD

Pacific Press® Publishing Association
Nampa, Idaho
Oshawa, Ontario, Canada
www.pacificpress.com

Cover design by Steve Lanto
Cover design resources from dreamstime.com
Inside design by Aaron Troia

Additional copies of this book may be purchased online at http://www.adventistbookcenter.com or by calling toll-free 1-800-765-6955.

Library of Congress Cataloging-in-Publication Data:

Fitzgerald, Troy, 1968-
  Live like you mean it : wisdom for the journey home / Troy Fitzgerald.
    p. cm.
  ISBN 13: 978-0-8163-2380-7 (paperback)
  ISBN 10: 0-8163-2380-1 (paperback)
  1. Bible. N.T. Peter, 2nd—Criticism, interpretation, etc. 2. Christian life—Biblical teaching. I. Title.
  BS2795.52.F58 2010
  227'.9306—dc22

                                                              2009047824

10 11 12 13 14 • 5 4 3 2 1

DEDICATION

This book is dedicated to Mary Lea, my neighbor, friend, and beloved artist whose storied life and unmistakable goodness has abundantly blessed me and my family over the seasons. She has taught me to savor each day with honesty and joy. Mary, thank you for years of friendship. It's good to know we are going home!

SPECIAL THANKS TO

My family, who continually deepens my understanding of God's grace and providence.

My good friend, Karl Haffner, who helped me learn to "storify" the journey home.

My friend, John Foote, dean of men at Walla Walla University, who now battles cancer. Your words and life have spoken irrevocably. The ripples and waves of your influence still speak to so many that we serve a mighty, good God.

My dear sister in Christ, Olive Hoehn, whose storied spiritual journey of faith, discovery, and devotion continues to bring joy and understanding to my life. Thank you, Olive, for your story.

Dr. Richard Davidson, professor at Andrews University Theological Seminary, for reminding me in class, through his books and speaking, and in various articles, that we are all a part of the exodus, the great journey to our Promised Land. The article "You Were There" came at just the right time! The last section of this book resonates with so much of what you have taught me that I wanted to include you as a partner.

Pacific Press® for the way you work so professionally, yet so clearly in step with the Spirit on projects that are truly making a difference in the world. I'm so proud to participate in God's work with you.

Finally, to our Lord Jesus Christ, who is preparing a place for us (John 14:1–3).

Contents

Start Walking Home

In a way, Pixar's story *Wall-E* is a tale about going home. The film features a solitary robot named Wall-E, who spent seven hundred years cleaning up garbage left behind by humans on an abandoned planet. Where are the humans? All the humans live on a large spaceship called the *Axiom,* which is parked on the outskirts of the galaxy, waiting for Earth to be cleaned up by robots. Originally, the ship had set out for a "five-year cruise" while the robots made the place livable again, but they lost track of the time. They had everything they needed in space. The years rolled by (seven hundred of them), and the captain is informed that Earth can be inhabited and it is time to go back home.

Home? For centuries the humans living on the ship thought that their life on board the *Axiom* was their destination. I chuckle at the silly depictions of humans in this story, but perhaps this animated film contains more truth than we might be comfortable with. Are we clinging to our lives on earth as if the here and now is all there is? The people on the *Axiom* were unaware of their true home and were completely unprepared to make their way home.

And then, there was an awakening—so simple and so real—but what emerged from that moment reoriented their thinking. Everything changed. Their destination became clear, and they finally got it and they made their way home.

We need an awakening—a wake-up call that urges us to our true home.

Aleck had such an awakening. As a child, he used to sit in the middle of a wheat field, earnestly trying to hear the wheat grow. Aleck's mother was almost totally deaf, and he spoke to her by pressing his lips to her forehead so she could feel the vibration of his words and better understand him. He discovered that when he spoke this way, the bones in his mother's forehead would resonate to the sound waves of his voice.

As a teenager, Aleck observed that a chord struck on one piano would cause the piano in another room to vibrate the same chord. For Alexander Graham Bell, it all came together later in his life, when all his ideas about sound waves, pitch, and electricity merged in a flash of insight from which he produced the telephone. For Aleck, everything changed as a result of his awakening.

Has that ever happened to you? Have you ever discovered a truth that so changed the way you think and live that it seemed impossible to forget and even more outrageous to ignore? Something like, that happened to me when I stumbled on Peter's second letter to the church. Struggling with doubt about my devotion to Christ, frustrated by the reality that I don't know how to change, and unsettled by the absence of peace about where I will spend eternity, I listened to Peter. He gets it. Peter's final thoughts on earth launched my first love experience; then the light came on, the fog lifted, and I started my walk home. Becoming a person whose focus is all about going home changes everything! The whole of Scripture screams this truth:

- There is no injustice or pain that life in heaven won't heal (Revelation 21:2–5; Romans 8:18).
- No joy or good experience on earth even compares to the bliss of eternal life (1 Corinthians 2:9).

- Nothing in this world has enough value to trade for the Promised Land (Mark 8:34; Matthew 13:44–46).

Peter knows all about going home and about the change that happens along the way. This disciple of Christ spent his final moments of life focused on eternity. We know Peter well, too well! Consider his résumé: A first-tier friend of Jesus. One of the inner circle. The first to speak up, step out, stab an ear, or start a fight. Peter is classic rock—Galilean style. "Little Rock" is a timeless status-quo shaker, risk taker, passionate promise maker. When his brother, Andrew, first introduced Peter to Jesus, the Savior looked at Peter and changed his name, saying, " 'You are Simon the son of John; you shall be called Cephas' (which is translated Peter)" (John 1:42, NASB). While Peter's name means "a little rock," he is more famous for bouncing back and forth between being a big talker and slow-and-stumbling walker. It is easy to admire his aspiration but equally nerve wracking when he opens his mouth or acts on his emotions.

Peter stood tall when he testified openly of Jesus, "You are the Christ, the Son of the living God" (Matthew 16:16, NASB) but fell hard when he gagged on Christ's words about His own death. The Lord rebuked Peter, saying, "Get behind me Satan" (verse 23, NASB). How do you go from a shameless belief in the Son of God, which "the gates of Hades will not overcome" (16:18) to being the very mouthpiece of Satan? How do you express such unmistakable loyalty and devotion by saying, "I will never deny You, I will even die with You" only to utter a few moments later, "I don't even know Him." Who would trust themselves after such a betrayal? How could you ever have confidence that you were a disciple? If Peter, after all the failure, could manage to still be confident about his walk to an eternal home, then why are we waiting to join him?

This book is for anyone whose walk with God can be described as:

- Up and down.
- One step forward and two steps back.
- Trying but getting nowhere.
- Going in circles.

Look to Peter for guidance because by the time he penned his last letter, we know where he began, how he walked, and where his journey was headed. Peter mastered the art of making his way home. Skip to the end of his letter and read a summary of Peter's final words on earth: "In keeping with his promise we are looking forward to a new heaven and a new earth, the home of righteousness. So then, dear friends, since you are looking forward to this, make every effort to be found *spotless, blameless* and *at peace* with him" (2 Peter 3:13, 14; emphasis added).

This book's title has a double meaning that echoes the theme of Peter's message as he writes his final words on earth. First, *Live Like You Mean It: Wisdom for the Journey Home* is about a journey, and it suggests the movement and purpose inherent in an ongoing process. Second, you can make your way (of life) all about "home." When heaven becomes your ultimate reference point, your choices, experiences, struggles, and opportunities fit marvelously into the course of each day. And each day brings you closer to home.

Three mind-sets

Live Like You Mean It: Wisdom for the Journey Home is divided into three sections that mirror pilgrims' mind-sets as they journey to the Promised Land.

Part 1: Start Home

"Grace and peace be yours in abundance through the knowledge of God and of Jesus our Lord. His divine power has given us everything we need for life and godliness through our knowledge of him who called us by his own glory and goodness. Through these he has given us his very great and precious promises, so that through them you may participate in the divine nature and escape the corruption in the world caused by evil desires" (2 Peter 1:2–4).

Being full of holes, tattered, or ragged is a reality that humanity misconstrues or ignores entirely. Obviously, how we understand this reality determines how we relate to our own sinful nature. There is a danger in not talking honestly about our reality because if we miss the truth about our desperate state, we dilute the truth about God's amazing provision through His grace. As we walk home, we need to take an honest look at our sin and the promise of salvation.

Part 2: Stride Home

Pilgrims must be earnest about practicing the character qualities of Christ. In the same way that every human home is marked with the attributes of the people who live there (warm, friendly, busy, stressed, quiet, controlling, open, neat, etc.), the home we travel to is shaped by the attributes of Christ. Furthermore, these qualities are woven into the character of every citizen as well as every pilgrim. There is system and style to how pilgrims make their way home. Peter urges, "For this very reason, make every effort to add to your faith goodness; and to goodness, knowledge; and to knowledge, self-control; and to self-control, perseverance; and to perseverance, godliness; and to godliness, brotherly kindness; and to brotherly kindness, love" (2 Peter 1:5–7).

Part 3: Storify How You Came to Make Your Way Home

Pilgrims are clear about being purposed for a different place than a sin-filled planet. By our relationship and our redemption, we walk home with 20/20 vision about where we are meant to be and how we are to get there. We join a procession of people whose storied lives continue to inspire and deepen our perception about going home. As we travel through our lives, we tell the story—the true story that we are a part of—about God and His people.

> For if you possess these qualities in increasing measure, they will keep you from being ineffective and unproductive in your knowledge of our Lord Jesus Christ. But if anyone does not have them, he is nearsighted and blind, and has forgotten that he has been cleansed from his past sins. Therefore, my brothers, be all the more eager to make your calling and election sure. For if you do these things, you will never fall, and you will receive a rich welcome into the eternal kingdom of our Lord and Savior Jesus Christ. So I will always remind you of these things, even though you know them and are firmly established in the truth you now have. I think it is right to refresh your memory as long as I live in the tent of this body, because I know that I will soon put it aside, as our Lord Jesus Christ has made clear to me. And I will make every effort to see that after my departure you will always be able to remember these things. We did not follow cleverly invented stories when we told you about the power and coming of our Lord Jesus Christ, but we were eyewitnesses of his majesty (2 Peter 1:8–16).

Eugene Peterson, in his timeless work *A Long Obedience in the Same Direction,* distinguishes two types of travelers: tourists and pilgrims. He states,

> Religion in our time has been captured by the tourist mind-set. Religion is understood as a visit to an attractive site to be made when we have adequate leisure. For some it is a weekly jaunt to church; for others, occasional visits to special services. . . . We go to see a new personality, to hear a new truth, to get a new experience and so somehow expand our otherwise hum-drum lives. The religious life is defined as the latest and the new-

est: Zen, faith healing, human potential, parapsychology, successful living, choreography in the chancel, Armageddon. We'll try anything—until something else comes along.[1]

I'm guilty of the tourist mind-set. I've wandered, backtracked, and chased after theological rabbits, and my closest friends would testify that I can rant with the best of ranters. But now, more than ever, I want to be going home. I want to be like those early Christians who truly lived like aliens, inhabiting this place, but loyal citizens of another land. I admire the pilgrim mind-set of the first- and second-century believers, who are described in *A Letter to Diognetus:*

> Christians are indistinguishable from other men either by nationality, language or customs. They do not inhabit separate cities of their own, or speak a strange dialect, or follow some outlandish way of life. Their teaching is not based upon reveries inspired by the curiosity of men. Unlike some other people, they champion no purely human doctrine. With regard to dress, food and manner of life in general, they follow the customs of whatever city they happen to be living in, whether it is Greek or foreign.
>
> And yet there is something extraordinary about their lives. They live in their own countries as though they were only passing through. They play their full role as citizens, but labor under all the disabilities of aliens. Any country can be their homeland, but for them their homeland, wherever it may be, is a foreign country.[2]

We need an awakening—a wake-up call that urges us along our pilgrim way. Are you ready to make your way home?

---

1. Eugene Peterson, *A Long Obedience in the Same Direction* (Downers Grove, Ill.: InterVarsity Press, 2000), 16.

2. "The Christians in the World," from a letter to Diognetus, http://www.vatican.va/spirit/documents/spirit_20010522_diogneto_en.html (accessed November 11, 2009).

Part 1: Start Home

Where do I start the walk home? In his second letter, Peter declares, "His divine power has given us everything we need for life and godliness through our knowledge of him who called us by his own glory and goodness. Through these he has given us his very great and precious promises, so that through them you may participate in the divine nature and escape the corruption in the world caused by evil desires" (2 Peter 1:3, 4).

Notice that each word or phrase in these verses is loaded with power.

His divine power. We can do nothing to merit God's mercy. In fact, the opposite is true for humanity—we are powerless. Paul echoes his agreement: "You see, at just the right time, when we were still powerless, Christ died for the ungodly" (Romans 5:6).

Has given. The action begins in the past tense but has continuing results. Count how many times a form of the word *give* appears in these two verses, and you'll see a pattern emerge. A gift can be desired, but not deserved. Wages are deserved. A reward is based upon merit. But a gift is only a gift if it is received as such.

Everything we need. Is there anything else? Of all the desires in this life, the human heart needs only one thing when offered the range of options—eternity.

Through our knowledge of him. John 17:3 claims that to know Christ is eternal life. While it may seem cliché—it is true—in fact, it is more than just true—it is Truth. We gain access to salvation through a relationship with Christ.

Promises. We need promises because we don't see the full results now. We have the promise from God that the gift is real. The faith we exercise in God's redemptive work for us is our method of receiving the gift. Because the promises are trustworthy, we can lean the full force of our weight on them and base our behavior and devotion on them.

Through these. Through trusting in the promises, we obtain possession of our inheritance.

Participate in the divine nature. We become one with Christ. We become collaborators in cooperation with Him. And if this is true, we have something to do!

Escape. What an amazing word in the Scriptures. The greatest escape of all was the Exodus. We must experience an exodus—the exodus! In order for us to escape, we must truly believe we are slaves in need of deliverance and that deliverance will finally come. Otherwise, without that assurance, our exodus becomes merely drudgery and a painful walk in the desert, with the Promised Land just beyond our reach.

Evil desires. The most evil desire known to man is a lust for self-exaltation. Part of receiving God's gift of grace is the recognition that we are sinful. Some prefer to call it "just being human," but such renaming of sin doesn't bring salvation any closer. In fact, the sooner we come to grips with how wrongheaded we are in our thinking and in our direction, the sooner we can embrace God's solution.

By looking at each word in the passage, we learn that eternal life is a gift that cannot be earned or deserved, but only received by faith in the promise that it is true. The first portion of this book focuses on the part of this walk during which we learn to receive the gift. We learn that only when we come to where our stubborn efforts end and God's mercy is accepted, then and only then, will we walk instead of wander.

As God reveals Himself to us through His Word and we come to sense our need for a Savior, we must accept a shift in thinking—a change of mind. But our thinking needs to be married to our experience. We need to make the confession—to hear our own voice say the words, *I'm lost, in need of help. Will You save me?* In this moment and from this moment of acknowledging our need of divine power, the gift is ours! Everything we need during our exodus will be provided. We are on our way to participating in the divine nature and becoming a new creation.

CHAPTER 1

Killer Cucumbers

Jesus had high expectations of Peter, and the brazen young fisherman knew it.

- I will make you a fisher of men.
- You are Peter and on this rock I will build My church, and the gates of hell will not overcome it.
- You will do even greater things than these when I go to the Father.

While Jesus set the bar high for Peter, He calls everyone to embrace their extraordinary calling as children of God. If the story of Christ had been written two thousand years later, the "little rock" could have easily have been Justin or Serena; and the same things He said to Peter, He could have said about you. Do you believe that? Truly, nothing else God says about the journey home will ever really make sense unless you accept the fact that you, a broken sinner, are also the indisputable heir of the King of heaven.

Ephesians 1:3, 4 declares, "Praise be to the God and Father of our Lord Jesus Christ, who has blessed us in the heavenly realms with every spiritual blessing in Christ. For he chose us in him before the creation of the world to be holy and blameless in his sight."

When Peter begins his letter by saying, "His divine power has given us everything we need for life and godliness through our knowledge of him who called us by his own glory and goodness" (2 Peter 1:3), the promise is not new, nor is it a joke. But your high calling comes to you in a world cloaked in darkness and eroded by corruption. That corruption is out there in the world, but it has infected every human heart with the disease of sin. *Sin.* The word means "to miss the mark." Another definition is "to aim too low."

In 1999, Monster.com, the online recruitment agency, aired the brilliant commercial "When I Grow Up," featuring children sharing their career dreams.

When I grow up,
- I want to claw my way up to middle management.
- I want to be a "yes man."
- I want to be underappreciated.
- I want to be paid less for doing the same job.
- I want to be replaced on a whim.
- I want to be forced into early retirement.

This ad's punch comes from the paradox: smiling, hopeful, idealistic kids with sweet voices announcing proudly their quest for mediocrity. And amid the humor, the truth slowly soaks in that what we say and do in life is so anemic, while what we all wish is for something amazing. We are constrained to say, "I want something greater." But the other voice inside our head whispers, "You don't deserve more." And both voices are true—but incomplete. As human beings, we are corrupted with sin from birth, and we deserve death as much as we deserve life. As human beings, we are also created in the image of God and possess an inherent desire for goodness. This war between two realities is what Paul meant by being "under sin."

According to Scripture, we are all "under sin" and born "into sin" (Romans 3:9, 23). Sin entered through Adam and Eve and brought condemnation and death to us all (5:12; 6:23). Sin is described as slavery, and such captivity leads to death (6:5, 6, 16–22). According the Bible, sin steals, kills, destroys, divides, infects, and condemns. Sin sneaks around in your heart and mind and stays alive, even when you think it might be dead. Sin starves you but trains you to eat the dirt, believing it is bread. Sin deceives you into a pattern of thinking that you can't be liberated, so you might as well marry your fate and try to like it.

The more you think about the horror of sin, the more you begin to hate it. The less you think about it, the more it creeps in and captivates, not only your life, but your belief about what constitutes life. I call it the "sindrome."

The sindrome

The dictionary defines *syndrome* as "a group of signs and symptoms that together are characteristic or indicative of a specific disease or other disorder" and "a group of things or events that form a recognizable pattern, especially of something undesirable."[1] Becoming aware of sin is not the only problem; what we believe about sin can also get us sidetracked. Make believing that sin is an inevitable reality only fosters a pattern of thought that numbs our consciences. But even when sin becomes popular, we have a sneaking suspicion that everyone at some point may sense, but hesitate to acknowledge it. It reminds me of something I read in *The Mole People*.

Below New York City live people who have, for one reason or another, chosen to dwell in the sewers. Jennifer Toth, a reporter, studied those who dwelt in the tunnels. In her book *The Mole People,* she cites an interchange with a man who let her interview him in exchange for a free lunch.

Flacko, a would-be leader of the underground, said,

"If I was in charge I'd put up a big sign on a platform saying, 'C'mon down! Everyone welcome! Come live free—rent free, tax-free, independent, free like Mandela!' " When he stops smiling, he turns earnest and leans over our table in the Chinese restaurant. . . . "If you write this book," he says, "you tell them the tunnels rob you of your life. No one should come down here. . . . Everyone down here knows it. They won't say it, but they know it."[2]

You can cling to the myth about life under the streets only if you refuse to think it through. The more you wonder and the more you examine, the more you see how wrongheaded the lie is. Listed below are a few myths about the nature of sin that people believe.

1. We are allowed one sin—one vice, because we are human. And if we are generally good in most areas of life, save our one precious sin, we should be fine. It really isn't fair to expect more of a person. This sense of entitlement first found its way into Lucifer's mind and became the very trademark of the devil's deception. Adam and Eve were taught by the snake that God had more for them but was holding back a portion of their entitlement.

2. We often simultaneously cherish sin and try to worship God—and believe that it is possible to succeed at both. Can we love sin and love God at the same time? Try telling your husband or your wife, "I love you, honey, but what you need to understand is that I'm also in love with her/him—it's complicated." What is complicated has to do with our notion of love. If we love our spouse, we exclude the possibility of loving anyone else that way.

3. We think that if we give in to the pleasures of the one sin that continually tempts us, and we satisfy our desire, we will get it out of our system. We pretend that after we give in to sin, we will eventually be willing to give it over to God in the end. The only way to think this way is to not think it through. Perhaps one of the sneakiest tricks Satan plays is making humanity believe we are smarter, wiser, and more clever than the snake. Not so. Giving in to sin only tightens the yoke of slavery.

4. *We often cherish the illusion that the passing of time cancels sin, some-what like smoke eventually blowing away into the atmosphere.* Key word—*illusion.* It's a trick Satan learned the hard way. If we fail to repent and deal with our selfishness, we have only the illusion that time has dissipated the problem. The truth remains—along with a truckload of guilt and disappointment.

5. *We often try to treat the disease of sin with an explanation, excuse, or with reason.* Perhaps some of the brightest people you know lie, cheat, betray, and destroy their lives and their homes by using their brainpower to brainwash away their sin.

As these assumptions ripen and bear fruit in our lives, we have a tendency to change the name of the sin in an attempt to camouflage the problem. Have you heard of the toothfish or rapeseed or prunes or the Chinese gooseberry or perhaps the dolphin fish? Probably not. In order to make the toothfish more palatable, they now called it the Chilean sea bass, which is likely to become extinct because of the high demand. The Canadians developed an edible oil from the rapeseed plant but had to rename it canola oil for people to purchase it. Because the name *prune* is inextricably tied to laxative, focus groups suggested calling the fruit dried plums when offered for sale in grocery stores. The Chinese gooseberry had its name officially changed to kiwifruit because of the striking resemblance to the New Zealand national bird (round, brown, and furry). And although restaurants touted the dolphin fish as a delicacy, nobody could choke down the notion of eating Flipper (even though dolphin fish are not related to dolphin mammals). So in the 1980s, restaurants starting using the Hawaiian name, *Mahi-mahi,* and profits soared. Some describe sin as "a broken relationship" or disobedience as a "failure to reach our true potential." I believe both definitions are true in part, but both tend to make sin seem more tolerable and less evil.

Calling adultery "a confusing phase" doesn't change the betrayal, only the name.

Fudging, stretching, misinforming, or telling only part of the truth doesn't change the intent to deceive. Call it what you like, it's a lie. Marsha Witten analyzed almost fifty taped sermons preached by Protestant pastors on the parable of the prodigal son. In her book *All Is Forgiven*, she observed an undeniable shift in the language chosen to describe sin. Witten reports, "As we have seen here, a closer examination of the sermons suggests the many ways in which the concept of 'sin' has been accommodated to fit secular sensibilities. For while some traditional images of sin are retained in this speech, the language frequently cushions the listeners from their impact, as it employs a variety of softening rhetorical devices."[3]

Not only do some change the name to make sin more palatable, but others change the subject to draw the attention away from the sin and focus on global problems that seem to be rampant, such as the failing economy or the deteriorating environment or political and social oppression. Clearly such issues are critical, but the sources of these problems are so various and vague that talking about them only distracts us from the salient truth: someone's sin caused this. It is also common to change the subject by focusing on individuals who are doing awful things that seem to loom larger than the speaker's own sin. Alcoholics might be tempted to counter their sin by saying, "Look, I have problems, but at least I'm not a pedophile like . . ." Jesus told a parable of the Pharisee and the tax collector. The tax collector, considered the "sinner," was keenly aware of his sin and asked for mercy, but the Pharisee failed to receive mercy because he acknowledged no problem and no need:

> Two men went up to the temple to pray, one a Pharisee and the other a tax collector. The Pharisee stood up and prayed about himself: "God, I thank you that I am not like other men—robbers, evildoers, adulterers—or even like this tax collector. I fast twice a week and give a tenth of all I get." But the tax collector stood at a distance. He would not even look up to heaven, but

beat his breast and said, "God, have mercy on me, a sinner." I tell you that this man, rather than the other, went home justified before God. For everyone who exalts himself will be humbled, and he who humbles himself will be exalted (Luke 18:10–14).

Another tactic is to change the rules by claiming, "It's not loving or grace oriented to talk about sin." The notion that feeling guilty, dirty, broken, lost, or bad can't be healthy may be a popular sentiment, but it is still untrue. I learned the value of truth-telling outside the principal's office (this time it wasn't me) as I eavesdropped on a disciplinary situation.

"Jeremy, what did you learn?" the seasoned principal asked of a boy who had bloodied the nose of a smaller classmate during recess.

Sobbing, the brokenhearted bully poured out his reply, "I'm so sorry. I got so mad at him and when I hit him, I knew I hurt him. It felt horrible. I'm so sorry. I feel sick. I just feel awful."

"Well I hope so, Jeremy," the principal added, "and I'm glad you feel sick because maybe you can see how wrong it is to hurt someone else. I hope you feel so bad your nose bleeds or even sense that boy's pain so much it makes you throw up." I heard the sound of an office garbage can being handed to the boy, "There, you can throw up in here if you like."

Jeremy sobbed but did not throw up. I started feeling sorry for the penitent bully. The principal believed that if Jeremy could taste how bad his sin really was, he might be more inclined to lean toward goodness instead of brutality. Even though the message seemed hard, communicating the truth about Jeremy's violence was an act of love and mercy.

Today, the cultural mood tends to move away from explicit truth-telling on the assumption that implicit hints about right and wrong are easier to hear. Change the name—and sin is not so wrong. Change the subject—and there are worse things to worry about. Change the rules—and it is no longer appropriate to talk about sin. Whether we are comfortable or not with the word *sin,* the truth remains—only by recognizing evil for what it really is can we even imagine or experience grace.

Perhaps the most frightening trend of all appears to be a diminished sense of the evilness of sin. If there is no sorrow for sin, there will be no joy in salvation. I believe this is why Paul said, "The wages of sin is death, but the gift of God is eternal life" (Romans 6:23). Sin and death that results from it are the extreme opposites of the gift of God's grace, which gives eternal life. Today people become squeamish when someone mentions the word *sin,* and the situation becomes even more awkward if sin is spoken of as evil.

Ellen White wrote prolifically about the nature of sin and the matchless love of God. The more you read her writings, the more uncomfortable you get with your sin, and the more you long to go home. Weaving God's Word with her insights in the book *Steps to Christ,* she points out the polarization between sin and Savior: "Behold Him in the wilderness, in Gethsemane, upon the cross! The spotless Son of God took upon Himself the burden of sin. He who had been one with God, felt in His soul the awful separation that sin makes between God and man. This wrung from His lips the anguished cry, 'My God, My God, why hast thou forsaken Me?' Matt. 27:46. It was the burden of sin, the sense of its terrible enormity, of its separation of the soul from God—it was this that broke the heart of the Son of God."[4]

When I read this passage, the contrast between heaven and hell become clearer. Puritan theologian John Owen once said, "The deceitfulness of sin is seen in that it is modest in its first proposals but when it prevails it hardens men's hearts, and brings them to ruin." As the heart hardens, it changes the standard for what constitutes sin and questions whether it is meaningful or not.

Killer cucumbers

A story is told about how fear seized a small town in the Midwest, when at night the sound of gunshots caused the people to quake with terror. In the morning, all over town there would be targets painted on cars, walls, and other public structures, with bullet holes at the center of the mark. The midnight sniper's dead aim stupefied local police and froze the townspeople with anxiety. The FBI was called in to investigate, and they eventually caught the sniper, but discovered that his skill as a marksman had been overestimated. After interrogating the perpetrator, they learned that the shooter would first fire the gun, then spray paint the target and place the bull's-eye around the bullet hole.

Human nature has discovered a way to remove sin—simply delete it from the conversation. Circle something else as an important target. If you aren't successful, change your aspirations to something less challenging. If the destination seems too far out of reach, choose an objective that is much more manageable. Lower the bar. Change the standard. Change the destination—then you can say you have arrived. You may have heard the popular saying, "Where you are is where you are supposed to be." The flaw in this thinking is equally clear: aiming for whatever seems doable will ultimately deceive you to death.

To illustrate the human tendency to detour after starting the walk home, remember Israel's complaint, even with the plagues and the Passover in the rearview mirror. In the wake of the parting of the Red Sea, the freshly liberated children of God experience hardship, and they want to turn back. As soon as the road to the Promised Land became narrow and long, many of the delivered Israelites wanted to go back to Egypt: "Now the rabble that was among them had a strong craving. And the people of Israel also wept again and said, 'Oh that we had meat to eat! We remember the fish we ate in Egypt that cost nothing, the cucumbers, the melons, the leeks, the onions, and the garlic. But now our strength is dried up, and there is nothing at all but this manna to look at' " (Numbers 11:4–6, ESV).

Cucumbers? They wanted cucumbers? Cucumbers provide virtually no nutrition; they are 96 percent water. God promised a land flowing with milk and honey (Exodus 3:17), but the food was not the reason to walk away from Egypt. They walked away from Egypt because they had been slaves and longed to be free. Cucumbers? Then they forgot everything God had already done to make this freedom real to them. "We want cucumbers!" They ignored the promise of a new life. "We want Egypt!" Why? Because they were hungry—hungry for cucumbers.

What happened? On their way to the Promised Land, they lost their sense of direction and ultimately their destination. Their hatred for slavery had softened, and their desire for freedom and the Promised Land had diminished. What did they have back in Egypt? Slavery, but they had food. Slavery, but they had houses. Slavery, but they had security. But dress up slavery any way you want it—it's still hell. It may become "good enough" if you take off your eyes off the Promised Land and the Promise Maker, but "good enough" still kills.

As long as you change the target—change the destination in your mind—you can make believe that bondage is liberty. Simply change the standard. Shoot for what you can hit; then draw a bull's-eye around it. And then hell becomes heaven—and the sneaky, nasty trick of sin is that you eventually believe it. When the sons of Eliab rebelled, they said, "Is it not enough that you have brought us up out of a land flowing with milk and honey to have us die in the wilderness" (Numbers 16:13, NASB).

They called *Egypt* the land of milk and honey! That is empty thinking—empty theology. Empty faith. It is banking on a loss and calling it a win. This hunger for cucumbers is a killer instinct. In the depths of our souls, we are hungry for something of substance, something that will satisfy our desire for life, the good life, the right life, the eternal life. We want freedom, but because we don't deserve it, we dismiss the possibility that Someone can liberate us. If this kind of thinking persists, without God's Word or someone shaking us out of the trance, we become like the monkeys John Maxwell describes from the following research project.

Four monkeys were placed in a room that had a tall pole in the center. Suspended from the top of that pole was a bunch of bananas. One of the hungry monkeys started climbing the pole to get something to eat, but just as he reached out to grab a banana, he was doused with a torrent of cold water. Squealing, he scampered down the pole and abandoned his attempt to feed himself. Each monkey made a similar attempt, and each one was drenched with cold water. After making several attempts, they finally gave up.

Then researchers removed one of the monkeys from the room and replaced him with a new monkey. As the newcomer began to climb the pole, the other three grabbed him and pulled him down to the ground. After trying to climb the pole several times and being dragged down by the others, he finally gave up and never attempted to climb the pole again.

The researchers replaced the original monkeys, one by one, and each time a new monkey was brought in, he would be dragged down by the others before he could reach the bananas. In time, the room was filled with monkeys who had never received a cold shower. Not one of them would climb the pole, but none of them knew why.[5]

This story is a commentary on being content to give up and still call it normal, when we suspect deep inside that there is more to life. God says to us all,

"Why do you spend your money on junk food,
    your hard-earned cash on cotton candy?
Listen to me, listen well: Eat only the best,
    fill yourself with only the finest" (Isaiah 55:2, *The Message*).

Jesus compelled the woman at the well to think it through: "Everyone who drinks of this water will thirst again; but whoever drinks of the water that I will give him shall never thirst; but the water that I will give him will become in him a well of water springing up to eternal life" (John 4:13, 14, NASB). The Promised Land continues to be a promise for us today as John encourages us on with a very specific, tangible promise in Revelation: "They will hunger no longer, nor thirst anymore; nor will the sun beat down on them, nor any heat; for the Lamb in the center of the throne will be their shepherd, and will guide them to springs of the water of life; and God will wipe every tear from their eyes" (Revelation 7:16, 17, NASB).

Treadmills or trailheads

Starting the walk home is likened to the difference between walking on a treadmill and stepping out at the trailhead. The treadmill is all about going nowhere but still getting tired. The trailhead is the launch point of an amazing journey. The treadmill tells how far you have gone. The trailhead takes you home. When you have finished your time on the treadmill, you still have a treadmill. When you have left the trailhead behind, you know you are on your way home.

Are you hungry for the abundant life? The real life? Do you want to start walking home? Peter believed, "Through these he has given us his very great and precious promises, so that through them you may participate in the divine nature and escape the corruption in the world caused by evil desires" (2 Peter 1:4). So, escape the treadmill of Egypt. The trailhead is the exodus. The only thing that will lift your eyes from Egypt is the belief in a Promised Land. Our escape starts with coming to the truth about ourselves. As God lifts our chin and says, "Do you want to go home?" we must come to believe that our desperate state of sin is not home. In *Steps to Christ*, we are reminded, "Would that all who have not chosen Christ might realize that He has something vastly better to offer them than they are seeking for themselves."[6]

We start by seeing sin for what it is and the promise of God's grace as real. Then we come to believe that we are children of God, captured and enslaved by evil. If not rescued, we will die. This is a simple description of sin, but as horrible as sin is, it is possible that we can get comfortable in our captivity. If you want to start walking home, first admit that you are not already there.

1. *Encarta World English Dictionary,* 1999, s.v. "syndrome."

2. Jennifer Toth, *The Mole People* (Chicago: Chicago Review Press, 1995), 288.

3. Marsha G. Witten, *All Is Forgiven: The Secular Message in American Protestantism* (Princeton, N.J.: Princeton University Press, 1993). See also "Preaching About Sin in Contemporary Protestantism," *Theology Today* 50: (July 1993).

4. Ellen G. White, *Steps to Christ* (Nampa, Idaho: Pacific Press® Publishing Association, 1954), 13.

5. John Maxwell, *Failing Forward: Turning Mistakes Into Stepping Stones for Success* (Nashville, Tenn.: Thomas Nelson, 2000), 47, 48.

6. White, 46.

Questions for Reflection

1. How would you describe the attitude people around you have toward sin today? Is it hated, downplayed, tolerated, or simply not talked about?

2. To what degree does desensitizing our idea of sin numb our understanding of grace?

3. This chapter discusses five myths about the nature of sin. Which of the five myths have you been especially tempted to entertain? Who in Scripture might have been tempted the same way?

4. In Numbers 11:4–6, the Israelites cry out for the comforts of Egypt (cucumbers). How do you explain this phenomenon?

5. When in your life have you felt like returning to the status quo?

6. In 2 Peter 1:4, Peter clearly is using the language of the exodus when he says, "He has given us very great and precious promises, so that through them you may participate in the divine nature and escape the corruption in the world" (emphasis added).

How would you rate your sensitivity to sin?					
1	2	3	4	5	6
hate					tolerance

7. A popular saying suggests that some people are so heavenly minded that they are no earthly good. In what sense is this true? How might this saying be incorrect? How might being oriented to the way home be a blessing to others?

Chapter 2

Making Change

I love my dog—regrettably. The truth is, I only pretend to not appreciate my pets. Although Dallas and Stella have done significant damage to my household, what they have destroyed pales in comparison to the disaster that happens when I try to fix what they have broken. It helps that they are cute, but I think I will name my next dog Repent. As much as I have had to yell, "Stella!" I'm convinced that I could get some kingdom mileage out of the deal by creating a dual purpose to my shouting. Imagine how effective it might be to bellow at my dog and simultaneously call people to turn from their sins and come to God, a bit like John the Baptist. Do you think it is worth a try? (I think it is amazing how my wife can shake her head and roll her eyes at the same time.) There are several flaws in this plan that my wife and everyone in my neighborhood are grateful for (1) My own dogs don't respond to any name I give them. They do what they want—so why would anyone else listen? (2) *Repent* is not a word or a concept that is widely understood. (3) I'm not John the Baptist.

Repent is a verb with an illusive quality to it. Like being on a teeter-totter, it is hard to find the balance between the mind and the actions. Is repentance something that starts in the mind and ends when the sinful action is avoided? If that is the case, I wonder if I have ever truly repented. Eugene Peterson claims that repentance is "a rejection that is also an acceptance, a leaving that develops into an arriving, a no to the world that is a yes to God."[1] Repentance may be a simultaneous experience (imperfect on both sides) that becomes deeper and more complete with experience.

When I was in the fifth grade, I became addicted to taking things apart. I took apart radios and eight-track tape players (a full description of this item is located in the appendix for those of you too young to know what I'm talking about). I honestly believed I could use the motor of a vacuum cleaner for a go-kart engine. The vacuum cleaner sounded so jetlike in contrast to go-karts, which back then were only glorified lawn-mowers. Sure you laugh, but I was dreadfully serious about finding a way to make an appliance into a vehicle. The answer was somewhere inside, and so I began to take the thing apart. Deeper and deeper, I made my way through the innards of the machine. I became quite skilled at unscrewing things, but alas, in the end I did not find a way to make a vacuum cleaner into a go-kart. Even more distressing, I had no idea how to turn the disassembled bucket of parts back into a vacuum cleaner again. So I hid the bucket of screws, wires, and unrecognizable parts behind our next-door neighbor's shed and hoped that that my parents would never feel the urge to vacuum anything, ever again. Sure enough, one day (the same day my parents felt the urge to vacuum something), Mr. Rob was cleaning behind his shed. Unbelievable. I found myself standing before my parents, who held out before me what used to be our vacuum cleaner, now a bucketful of parts. My explanations and my excuses were desperate attempts to cover my sin. Finally, I admitted what was obvious to everyone, my "holeyness."

Owning my shameful act felt awful—horrible, but even though my parents disciplined me, there was freedom in the truth. In the same way that confession is both scary and liberating, the whole notion of facing your sin causes your heart to resist, dig in, or distract. But it is the only way. Recognizing our "holeyness"—the state in which we discover that "all our righteous acts are like filthy rags"—brings us to a fork in the road where we have a choice to make about our sin problem. Something needs to change. And in a world that tends to change the name, change the subject, or change the rules, God calls us to repent—to change our minds.

After Peter got it, he preached a sermon that pricked to the core those who heard it. The listeners asked, "What do we do?" They were essentially asking, "Where do we start?" Peter replied, "Repent and be baptized, every one of you, in the name of Jesus Christ for the forgiveness of your sins" (Acts 2:38). The word *repent* means to change your mind in such a way that it changes your behavior. What needs to change? Peter would say, "Your mind—so much so that you walk differently."

True repentance is changing the mind and your direction. It is like the boy who got his hand stuck in the candy jar, sneaking something sweet while his parents were not paying attention. His parents tried using soapsuds, lotion, and baby oil, but at last they came to the point where they decided to break the ceramic jar because it seemed the only way to free his hand. Just when they were about to smash the jar, the boy cried out, closing his eyes, "Would it help if I let go of the candy?" The genius of that story is that it reveals both parts of repentance: the mind and the will to change.

Because the problem with sin is an issue of the heart, the change required must go deep, to the very things that motivate and foster our selfishness. In David's song, you can see an example of true repentance and confession. As the king, David could have not only renamed his behavior with Bathsheba but made up an entire new vocabulary justifying it. David might have drawn attention to greater vices taking place in the kingdom or even focused on all the good that he had done up to that point. He could have simply silenced any suggestion that his behavior was wrong.

Sometimes, we can know we are broken, but because we don't look at the whole story—we focus on the act of sin and not the source. For such a problem we need a revelation. The prophet Nathan knew by divine revelation that David could not see clearly and needed some help clarifying the problem and so he told David the following story.

> "There were two men in a certain town, one rich and the other poor. The rich man had a very large number of sheep and cattle, but the poor man had nothing except one little ewe lamb he had bought. He raised it, and it grew up with him and his children. It shared his food, drank from his cup and even slept in his arms. It was like a daughter to him. Now a traveler came to the rich man, but the rich man refrained from taking one of his own sheep or cattle to prepare a meal for the traveler who had come to him. Instead, he took the ewe lamb that belonged to the poor man and prepared it for the one who had come to him" (2 Samuel 12:1–4).

Notice in the murderous, adulterous king's response to Nathan's parable how keen and effective storytelling can be. "David burned with anger against the man and said to Nathan, 'As surely as the LORD lives, the man who did this deserves to die! He must pay for that lamb four times over, because he did such a thing and had no pity' " (verses 5, 6).

Wait for it. The storyteller has not failed in his attempt to bring David around. The process is just getting started. The horror of sin and the need for justice has to fully blossom for the stubborn heart to break. David first has to witness the truth about sin's effects before he can apply it to his own scenario. He also has to make a verbal, public confession as to how wrong this wickedness truly is. He, as the king, has the final word. So, having called sin by its right name, Nathan asks, "Why did you despise the word of the LORD by doing what is evil in his eyes? You struck down Uriah the Hittite with the sword and took his wife to be your own. You killed him with the sword of the Ammonites" (verse 9).

When we come to the end of our arguments, the end of our excuses, we face our holeyness with one of two responses: honesty or denial. Honesty accepts the truth and looks for help; denial fears the truth because it doesn't believe there is help. If there is only one thing David knew in the basement of his shame, it was the truth that there is One who can and will help. The loud cry of those who know David's plight and have found freedom in God's grace should be, "There is help! There is a promise of a Helper, Liberator, Savior, and Redeemer."

I sat with a friend in the doctor's office to hear the results of some tests he had gone through. He heard the bad news first: "This kind of tumor in your brain will kill you," the doctor stated. "What are my options?" my friend asked. Some might question the diagnosis; that would be normal. But at some point after we learn the truth about ourselves, we must ask, "What are my options?" The doctor offered hope in one sentence: "Now, it is risky, but there is a way to remove the tumor." The amazing work of hope has a way of enabling us to own our problem, when there is a way. David knew of God's way to save sinners, so David made his confession to the prophet Nathan, "I have sinned against the LORD" (2 Samuel 12:13).

If you need to hear the full story of David's repentance (and we all do), he wrote it in a song found in Psalms 51.

Have mercy on me, O God,
　　according to your unfailing love;
according to your great compassion
　　blot out my transgressions.
Wash away all my iniquity
　　and cleanse me from my sin.
For I know my transgressions,
　　and my sin is always before me.
Against you, you only, have I sinned
　　and done what is evil in your sight,

so that you are proved right when you speak
> and justified when you judge.

Surely I was sinful at birth,
> sinful from the time my mother conceived me.

Surely you desire truth in the inner parts;
> you teach me wisdom in the inmost place.

Cleanse me with hyssop, and I will be clean;
> wash me, and I will be whiter than snow.

Let me hear joy and gladness;
> let the bones you have crushed rejoice.

Hide your face from my sins
> and blot out all my iniquity.

Create in me a pure heart, O God,
> and renew a steadfast spirit within me.

Do not cast me from your presence
> or take your Holy Spirit from me.

Restore to me the joy of your salvation
> and grant me a willing spirit, to sustain me (verses 1–12).

We can be holy only when we first embrace the truth that we are holey. The beauty of this genuine repentance is that when we face the truth, we also face the One who is the Truth—and He has promised to save us. Perhaps the complicated moments in our lives occur at the place where we must admit our sins and believe Jesus when He says, "If we confess our sins, he is faithful and just and will forgive us our sins and purify us from all unrighteousness" (1 John 1:9).

"Come now, let us reason together,"
> says the LORD.

"Though your sins are like scarlet,
> they shall be as white as snow;

though they are red as crimson,

    they shall be like wool" (Isaiah 1:18).

"Therefore, if anyone is in Christ, he is a new creation; the old has gone, the new has come!" (2 Corinthians 5:17). "For God so loved the world that he gave his one and only Son, that whoever believes in him shall not perish but have eternal life" (John 3:16). From sin to righteousness, from death to life, red like crimson to white as snow—the old has gone and the new has come.

The distinctions are stark. David, confronted by the full effect of his sin, faced the options before him and made the choice to surrender. Ellen White describes David's response in *Steps to Christ:* "The prayer of David after his fall, illustrates the nature of true sorrow for sin. His repentance was sincere and deep. There was no effort to palliate his guilt; no desire to escape the judgment threatened, inspired his prayer. David saw the enormity of his transgression; he saw the defilement of his soul; he loathed his sin. It was not for pardon only that he prayed, but for purity of heart. He longed for the joy of holiness—to be restored to harmony and communion with God."[2]

Peter knew the story of David and the king's journey to learn to hate sin and love God's mercy. Like it or not, Peter is famous, not for his letters or even his devotion to Christ, but for his sin, his betrayal. But just prior to the moment of Peter's disloyalty, Jesus had warned the disciples, "This very night you will all fall away on account of me" (Matthew 26:31). Peter takes the rap for being the one who choked on his empty promises, but all the disciples failed. But Jesus looked at Peter and said, "I tell you the truth, . . . this very night, before the rooster crows, you will disown me three times" (verse 34).

"But Peter declared, 'Even if I have to die with you, I will never disown you.' And all the other disciples said the same" (verse 35). Everyone jumped on board the promise-maker train that night—not just Peter. But Peter believed he would keep his promise. The Bible says that "Peter followed him at a distance, right up to the courtyard" (verse 58). Peter followed Christ as far as his faith would go; only he thought his faith would have gone further. How many of us are surprised by our failure to stay true. We make promises, and we truly, earnestly believe at the moment that we can keep them—but we can't. When we fail to acknowledge the full effects of sin that lurk in us, we are tempted to believe the lie that we are able to be true. However, Jesus, fully aware of humanity's overestimated devotion, as well as our underestimated notion of sin, still made the following promise: "Simon, Simon, Satan has asked to sift you as wheat. But I have prayed for you, Simon, that your faith may not fail. And when you have turned back, strengthen your brothers" (Luke 22:31, 32).

Oh, if we all could take in God's confidence in us. If we could only see how God believes in us, we could truly put our trust in Him. The key word in Jesus' promise to Peter is *when* not *if.* Jesus didn't say, "If you turn your ship around and get on the right course," but rather, "When you discover the end of your devotion and the range of your sin, you will repent and be converted." So will everyone else who chooses to believe the promise of redemption.

Let's summarize. The walk home to eternity begins with our understanding that we are not home now—home is where God leads us by His grace. We must understand the true nature of sin in order to experience the good grace of God. Avoiding all the tricks and traps of Satan's lying ways, we come to admit that we are lost, trapped, and enslaved by sin. We need an exodus, a Liberator, a Redeemer. Repentance is the first step on the trailhead home. Repentance is a change of mind that leads to a new direction in life. The new life or the destination we are headed toward is a promise given by God, and we believe that word by faith with each step we take toward home.

---

1. Eugene Peterson, *A Long Obedience in the Same Direction,* 33.
2. Ellen G. White, *Steps to Christ,* 24, 25.

Questions for Reflection

1. When in your life have you felt a real heart sorrow for your sin?

2. Eugene Peterson defines repentance as "a rejection that is also an acceptance, a no to the world that is a yes to God." If this definition is accurate, what specifically do you need to say Yes to as well as what you should say No to?

3. As you look at David's experience with repentance, why do you think Nathan revealed his sin through a story? How does David's repentance in Psalm 51 demonstrate the marks of true repentance?

4. In Luke 22:31, 32, Jesus warns Peter about the blind spot in the brazen disciple's character: "Satan has asked to sift you as wheat, but I have prayed for you . . . that your faith may not fail. And when you have turned back, . . ." Jesus announces that Peter will fail, but is confident that Peter will turn around. Who in your life has known the truth about you but still believes the best? How does that person's confidence in you impact your life?

5. A quotation from *Steps to Christ* states, "There are many who fail to understand the true nature of repentance. Multitudes sorrow that they have sinned, and even make an outward reformation because they fear that their wrongdoing will bring suffering upon themselves. But this is not true repentance in the Bible sense. They lament the suffering, rather than the sin" (23). How is this true for you?

6. Today, try to take a few moments to reflect on the sinfulness of sin and how it has affected your life, but also meditate on how amazing the grace of God really is.

CHAPTER 3

Un-deceiving and Re-minding

When I taught high school, I became keenly aware of the way young people developed the skill of manipulation as though it were a biochemical result of adolescence. Once I needed a few items from the grocery store, and four young men rode with me. Right now you should be saying, "Oh no, this can't end well."

As we made our way past the bakery, one of the students cried out, "Dad, you said we could have doughnuts if we did our chores!" I sent him an icy glare to calm him down, but he continued. "You are not going to lie to us again, are you? You said we could have doughnuts!" The others took the cue and came in for the kill, all chiming in, "You promised, Dad," and "Are you going to break your promises to us again?" and "You never keep your promises."

Now most of the people in the store witnessing this charade did the math and grew suspicious as to how a twenty-five-year-old man could have sired four teenage boys and still have the courage to take them all to the store together. For most, it was highly improbable. Others were not so quick with math, but were quick to judge. Some shook their heads in disapproval. Others glared poniards into my face. Those young monsters jammed me and ultimately got their doughnuts.

After we had piled into the van, I looked in my rearview mirror at them and asked, "Hey guys, are the doughnuts good?" They mumbled and chuckled their approval. I added, "Nice work, guys. Enjoy the doughnuts; you paid a very high price for them." I, eventually and appropriately, exacted revenge, but what I remembered most was how the people around the store reacted so viscerally to the accusation, "You never keep your promises." Promises are sacred.

Promises. Promises. According to Peter, the doorway to our eternal home is through a promise and ultimately through the One who is the Promise. The word *promise* has several definitions:

1. To assure somebody that something will certainly happen or be done.
2. To pledge to somebody to provide or do something.
3. To cause somebody to expect something.
4. To assure or warn somebody that something is true or inevitable.

When we apply these verbs (*assure, pledge, expect*) to our belief that God is able to save us, then we begin the process of undeceiving ourselves—of changing our minds. James, not the apostle, but a sixth-grader in my Bible class, used the word *un-deceive* after reading the story of Adam and Eve. "Adam and Eve got deceived and afterward had to get undeceived so they could believe God again." I looked down at the floor and studied James's shoes, which always seemed to be a tangled mess of knots. Immediately, the word picture of untying those laces partnered with the work of "undeceiving." I had to bring it up. His face slowly formed a pained expression at the idea of unimaginable time and effort it would take to untie all of the knots. I think young James described quite efficiently the human struggle to change the way we think about God and His promises for sinful humanity. We need to be "un-deceived" but also "re-minded," as Romans 12:2 puts it: "Do not conform any longer to the pattern of this world, but be transformed by the renewing of your mind. Then you will be able to test and approve what God's will is—his good, pleasing and perfect will."

In order to start making your way home, you must reject the lie (un-deceive) and believe the promise (re-mind). "Do not be conformed," Paul warns. The lie is that there is no way out of our sin other than what we might do for ourselves. If we don't untie the lie and un-deceive the problem, then we will come to accept the hopelessness and simply live with it. Paul then adds, "Be transformed by the renewing of your mind." Re-mind. The promise God makes is that He has made an escape through His Son. Do you believe it? Practicing belief and expressing confidence, at whatever level we experience it, is the starting point for re-minding. But perhaps believing a promise is harder than it would seem.

In this age, people are typically cynical about promises. Products are advertised to make a person thinner, smarter, healthier, irresistible, and rich—all in the comfort and privacy of your own home. A new life, body, and wealth await you—only one phone call or click away. The Web site ScamBusters.org listed the top ten work-at-home scams that target people who long for this promise of wealth to be real. Assembling toys or crafts at home might seem easy in theory. What could be complicated about that? Simply get the parts and instructions and later return the assembled item for a ridiculously higher price than the price of the kit. What's the catch? *You buy the kit* of stuff that needs to be assembled. ScamBusters.org revealed that once you buy, assemble, and return the product for your paycheck, your work is systematically rejected because it "does not meet the company's specifications." Getting your money back is nearly impossible. Medical billing, e-mail processing, and typing at home are samples of many scams that claim you can make thousands of dollars at home.

One particular scam tempts you with the promise of quick cash and prompts you to call 1-900 . . . for more information. The 900 call costs the caller, and there is no recovery or recourse for the money you lose. Promise big. Deliver nothing. And people feel too ashamed to fight back, so they simply eat the loss and learn (ideally). During the Great Depression, the envelope-stuffing scam wreaked havoc on hopeful people looking to put food on the table during seriously troubled times. This classic work at home opportunity was replaced by the Internet, which has sucked millions from people desperately trying to find an easy way to make money.

People seem to have an inherent desire to believe that someone out there wants to give them "the promised land" out of the kindness of their hearts. If money, health, or love were that easily made with equal benefit to all—well, let's be realistic, would you even have to advertise?

Peter reminds us that the only way home is through a promise made by God: "Through these he has given us his very great and precious promises, so that through them you may participate in the divine nature and escape the corruption in the world caused by evil desires" (2 Peter 1:4).

What are the promises of God worth to you today? Are believers motivated more by the life that is now than by the life to come? Where is there reward here on earth? In a wedding ceremony, the vows are the crucial part of the service. The music, the kiss, the candles, the laughing or crying are all important elements, but the exchange of vows or promises are the nonnegotiable part of what constitutes a wedding. Furthermore, keeping their promises are what makes the couple a husband and wife; this is called marriage. Keeping your promise and trusting that someone else will keep theirs are two different experiences. I've often thought that keeping a promise is easier than trusting that someone else will keep theirs. Herein lies the human conundrum: can we, do we, trust that God will be true to His promises? Sweeping through a small book entitled *Bible Promises,* I felt my right eyebrow elevate involuntarily at bold claims God has made in the Scripture.

In Isaiah 43:2, God promised,

When you pass through the waters,

I will be with you;
and when you pass through the rivers,
    they will not sweep over you.
When you walk through the fire,
    you will not be burned;
    the flames will not set you ablaze.

I'm sure there are martyrs who either burned at the stake or drowned, knowing that God made this promise. Would they say God is true to His word? Since we can't interview them, we must assume that Christian martyrs stood faithfully on the promise that God would keep His word to them.

Where is God when tragedy strikes? Answer: Close. Probably closer than anyone really is aware. Psalm 34:18 claims, "The LORD is close to the brokenhearted and saves those who are crushed in spirit." David's promise about God is similar to the promise Jesus makes about the times when we feel alone because of persecution. He states, "Are not two sparrows sold for a penny? And not one of them will fall to the ground apart from your Father. But even the hairs of your head are all numbered" (Matthew 10:29, 30, ESV). The more accurate translations describe God as being with us during this season. In Scripture, God never promises more than He can deliver, but His promises tend to be couched in reality.

For example, we love the promise found in Jeremiah 29:11 " 'I know the plans I have for you,' declares the LORD, 'plans to prosper you and not to harm you, plans to give you hope and a future.' " Don't be seduced by focusing only on the sweet part of this promise. The context of God's extremely positive vow is mixed with a seventy-year sabbatical of slavery in Babylon. This promise is not only a promise to prosper Israel, but a prophecy that they would re-learn or get un-deceived back into real devotion to God alone.

Perhaps my favorite promise of all is found in John 11:25, 26, where Jesus spoke to Martha and Mary as they grieved the death of their brother,

Lazarus: "I am the resurrection and the life. He who believes in me will live, even though he dies; and whoever lives and believes in me will never die. Do you believe this?" I find myself repeating the question, often paraphrasing it in my mind, "You know me and you know that I would not lie. Will you stand on this promise?"

Clearly, Jesus is not simply offering a promise to escape the permanence of death; He offers so much more—eternal life. John said, "And this is what he promised us—even eternal life" (1 John 2:25). And when we read these promises from God's Word, they ring with the assumption that God keeps His promises. The author of Hebrews captures the first work of making our way home, urging believers with a challenge: "Let us hold unswervingly to the hope we profess, for he who promised is faithful" (Hebrews 10:23).

And there it is! God makes promises, but then His biggest promise is the Person of His Son. And in the same way that "in the beginning was the Word . . . and the Word became flesh" (John 1:1, 14), so it is that in the Old Testament God made promises—and then He became the Promise of eternal life.

Notice how Joshua, in the sunset of his career, offers a big-picture reminder to the people: "Now I am about to go the way of all the earth. You know with all your heart and soul that not one of all the good promises the LORD your God gave you has failed. Every promise has been fulfilled; not one has failed" (Joshua 23:14). Moreover, Paul synthesizes the plural "promises" mentioned hundreds of times in the Bible into one bold, beautiful promise:

> As surely as God is faithful, our message to you is not "Yes" and "No." For the Son of God, Jesus Christ, who was preached among you by me and Silas and Timothy, was not "Yes" and "No," but in him it has always been "Yes." For no matter how many promises God has made, they are "Yes" in Christ. And so through him the "Amen" is spoken by us to the glory of God.

Now it is God who makes both us and you stand firm in Christ. He anointed us, set his seal of ownership on us, and put his Spirit in our hearts as a deposit, guaranteeing what is to come (2 Corinthians 1:18–22).

For those who step out and make their way home, the start is perhaps the hardest part of the journey. It's not always as easy to believe the promise in practice as it is in theory. In fact, walking as though the promise of God is real is something we learn as we go. But we must start. And even though the world has trained us to be competent, self-sufficient thinkers who don't get sold a promise until we have sufficient proof, we are still invited to walk home. And there are many who become un-deceived about their self-sufficiency and get re-minded about their Savior's promise. One example that comes to mind is the man who gave us the hymn "Standing on the Promises."

Standing on the promises of God

Russell Kelso Carter stood tall as a competent man, who seemingly could do anything he set his mind to. The guy was a one-man talent festival. Born in 1849, Carter lived to be almost eighty years old—but his long life paled in comparison to the kinds of things he was able to accomplish. Carter was known to be an amazing athlete in his years as a student. He became a professor of chemistry, natural science, civil engineering, and mathematics. Add to the list successful sheep rancher, publisher of textbooks, as well as the author of several novels. He became a Methodist minister and a pivotal leader in the Holiness Movement camp meetings during the latter part of the nineteenth century. He also studied medicine and became a physician. Not the least of his endeavors was the compilation of a hymnal for the Christian and Missionary Alliance, to which he contributed sixty-eight original tunes and fifty-two poems. If anyone had a leg to stand on it was Russell Kelso Carter—the personification of competence. Yet it is likely that his most significant contribution was a hymn he wrote about trusting the competence of Christ alone. Read a few stanzas and you'll recognize the military cadence of "Standing on the Promises."

Standing on the promises of Christ my King
Through eternal ages let His praises ring,
Glory in the highest, I will shout and sing,
Standing on the promises of God.

Chorus:
Standing, standing,
Standing on the promises of God my Saviour,
Standing, standing,
I'm standing on the promises of God.

Standing on the promises that cannot fail,
When the howling storms of doubt and fear assail,
By the living Word of God I shall prevail,
Standing on the promises of God.

Standing on the promises of Christ the Lord,
Bound to Him eternally by love's strong cord,
Overcoming daily with the Spirit's Sword,
Standing on the promises of God.

Standing on the promises I cannot fall,
Listening every moment to the Spirit's call,
Resting in my Saviour as my all in all,
Standing on the promises of God.

When the hymn was first published, the song had five stanzas, but the last has been omitted in the more recent versions:

Standing on the promises I now can see
Perfect present cleansing in the blood for me;
Standing in the liberty where Christ makes free,
Standing on the promises of God.

Some of us are not in danger of self-reliance the way Carter might have been tempted. But the promise of God's redemption and the reality of the Promised Land anchored him deep in the grace of God. Don't you want to believe that you are going home? Don't you want to know that it is certain? Can't you feel your own desire for assurance that this is the way home? I know I want, more than anything else, to make "going home" the theme of my life.

Popular movies are filled with stories of dads who continually break their promises to their kids in an effort to achieve personal goals. Movies such as *The Hero, Mrs. Doubtfire,* and *Liar Liar,* each portray the heartbreak children experience when their father fails to show up at games, parties, and performances. Relentlessly, the children still try to believe their dad will come through. I believe there is something wired deep in the human heart that wants to believe that a promise made is a promise kept. The sacredness of God's promise to us lives in us. To remind yourself about the promise, sing about it. Practice saying out loud, "God's promise to us is true." Speak to God in prayer and remind Him about His promise to you. He has not forgotten it, but He wants you to be re-minded.

Questions for Reflection

1. Think about the most important promises that other people have made to you. What are the elements or foundation pieces of such promises? How does your experience with the promises made or broken shape the way you see the promises God has for you in Scripture?

2. If you could un-deceive yourself of one lie, what would it be? Why? If you could re-mind or re-train your mind to believe a truth that is hard to accept, what would that truth be?

3. In 2 Peter 1:4, Peter claims that "the escape" or the way home is through the promises God has made to save humanity. In a practical sense, how often does this promise of an eternal home come to play throughout the course of an ordinary day? How do you think your days might be different if you could re-mind yourself of the promises God has made?

4. How are the promises made as marriage vows like the promises God has made to His children? How are they different?

5. Several promises from Scripture are cited in this chapter. Which promise especially speaks to you today? Why?

6. This week, place before you in a tangible way some of the most precious promises you know from Scripture. Print them out, write them down, or simply leave the Bible open to that particular promise throughout each day and see how re-minding yourself about home helps you on your journey.

CHAPTER 4

The Question:
Do You Want to Go Home?

I trust you have heard well-meaning people say, "There is no such thing as a dumb question." Well, they are wrong. For example, "What was the best thing *before* sliced bread?" or "What do you call a male ladybug?" and "Why are violets blue and not violet?" So perhaps the above inquiries are not "dumb questions" as much as they are meaningless curiosities. Nevertheless, questions prompt our thinking with either meaningful content or mindless information.

I once had a teacher who believed that journaling was the most efficacious learning activity in which students could engage. I hate journaling. I'm sure it's good for you—the same way spinach is—and journaling engages my gag reflex in a similar manner as spinach does. So I would test my teacher to see (1) if she was even reading my deep ruminations, and (2) if I could drive her crazy with my senselessness. She would say, "Just write what you are thinking when you think about what we are talking about in class." She was a rookie teacher. Because she failed to give specific prompts for our journaling, I would dream up questions from the depth of my senselessness to be the fodder for my journal entries. Here are some of my deep questions that would prompt my journaling.

1. Why isn't *phonetic* spelled the way it sounds?
2. Why are there interstate highways in Hawaii?
3. If nothing sticks to Teflon, how do they make Teflon stick to the pan?
4. Why is it that when you transport something by car, it's called a shipment, but when you transport something by ship, it's called cargo? I don't understand.
5. When I see a sign at Taco Bell that reads "Drive Through Window," I wonder, *Are they serious?*
6. I often wonder what good does a falling rock sign do? How are we supposed to drive differently?
7. Why isn't evaporated milk a gas?
8. Why are all calico cats female? Ordinarily, male cats have XY chromosomes, while females have XX. The X chromosomes carry the genes for coat colors. Therefore, female cats inherit their coat color—nevermind.
9. How do figure skaters keep from becoming dizzy while spinning?
10. Why is there no Betty Rubble character in Flintstones multivitamins? There is a Flintmobile, Dino, Bamm-Bamm, Wilma, Barney, Pebbles, and of course, Fred, but no Betty. What dark secret hides behind this clever ruse?

Later in life I tried to contact my English teacher to apologize, but she had retired from a career as an educator at the ripe old age of twenty-six. The point is that my questions were as meaningless as the answers. So much of our lives is spent answering meaningless questions. Knowing what we know about the darkness of sin and glory of God's love for us, what then becomes the guiding question for our lives? Do we even know what it is or should be?

It's likely that we don't think about our questions at all; we just live. But our living is still guided by something, even if it is the random unchecked beliefs that lie under the surface of our minds. However, there is one question that most everyone considers. In every culture and with almost every religion, in some form, one faces the question of eternal life. For Christians, eternal life in our home with God is our reason for the journey. Let's be honest, we are in it for the reward. At best, we want to live with our Savior throughout eternity! At bare minimum, we don't want to die and miss heaven, but in many cases, we simply don't want to experience hell.

However, in the Bible, the rewards of eternal life and Christ are inseparable. We cannot imagine one without the other. Christ repeatedly reminds those of us who are on the walk home to pay attention to the rewards, indeed, to even be motivated by and think often about the rewards. See for yourself:

- See, the Sovereign LORD comes with power, and his arm rules for him. See, his reward is with him, and his recompense accompanies him (Isaiah 40:10).
- "Rejoice and be glad, because great is your reward in heaven" (Matthew 5:12).
- "If anyone gives even a cup of cold water to one of these little ones because he is my disciple, I tell you the truth, he will certainly not lose his reward" (Matthew 10:42).
- "The Son of Man is going to come in his Father's glory with his angels, and then he will reward each person according to what he has done" (Matthew 16:27).
- "Rejoice in that day and leap for joy, because great is your reward in heaven" (Luke 6:23).
- "Love your enemies, do good to them, and lend to them without expecting to get anything back. Then your reward will be great, and you will be sons of the Most High" (Luke 6:35).
- Whatever you do, work at it with all your heart, as working for the Lord, not for men, since you know that you will receive an

inheritance from the Lord as a reward (Colossians 3:23, 24).

- He regarded disgrace for the sake of Christ as of greater value than the treasures of Egypt, because he was looking ahead to his reward (Hebrews 11:26).
- "Behold, I am coming soon! My reward is with me, and I will give to everyone according to what he has done" (Revelation 22:12).

The reward is real. Such a desire for the reward compelled two men on two different occasions to come to Christ with the same question, "What must I do to inherit eternal life?" Now *that* is a meaningful question! Some may answer by saying, "The question is faulty—there is nothing anyone can do to merit salvation." True, but that isn't the question—the question has to do with inheriting, not with meriting. There are two ways to become an heir—by adoption or by birth. God does not give eternal life to people who don't believe in and receive the gift (John 1:12; 3:16). So let's paraphrase their question and ask, "How do I become an heir to Christ and fully obtain the right to eternal life with Him?"

The first encounter is between Jesus and the expert in the law. To simply say "a lawyer" doesn't accurately convey the gravity of this scene. He wasn't just "a lawyer" but an expert in the law of God. Other than the Author Himself, few would have known the law better than this man. It is important to note that the mood of this exchange is key to understanding the lawyer's motives. The Bible says that he asked this question to "test" Jesus (Luke 10:25). The spirit of this encounter was thoughtful and earnest. But the very question demonstrates that the rabbis of that time taught that eternal life was a reward to be earned through effort.

Clearly, the prejudice of the Jewish leaders and their self-righteousness prompted Jesus to tell the story of the good Samaritan to answer the question. Permit me to paraphrase Jesus' answer: "You desire eternal life, but you love your self-righteousness, and you hate the Gentiles more than you treasure heaven. If you want to inherit eternal life, then want it enough to become an agent of mercy to everyone. You will have to trade in your hatred. You will have to humble yourself and be a child of God like the rest of us, all of us—including Samaritans."

The second encounter is with the rich young ruler (Mark 10:17–31). Like the lawyer, his motives seem pure and his desire appears genuine. His sincerity moves Jesus to a unique response: "Jesus looked at him and loved him" (Mark 10:21). But Jesus knew the deceitfulness of riches—a spell so powerful that you can live well and right, but still deny the truth that you love more than anything else. So, to paraphrase the answer: "When I look at you, I see a genuine heart for God. I want to grant you your heart's desire, but we both know that you love your wealth more than you love heaven. But trust Me, give Me a try, take a leap of faith and be willing to let go of your money—and you won't regret it. You will feel your desire for heaven grow even stronger and your love of money weaken."

Sadly, both men seem to go away with a lot to think about, but no choice to become heirs of eternal life. Strangely enough, the promise of heaven, as great as it is, did not seem to be enough to compel them to choose to start the walk home. If they had chosen to follow Christ, they would have spoken their confession and started the walk home.

Peter did this part well—he always made a public speech that accompanied his public stand. More often than not, Peter, even before he had clearly thought through his convictions, boldly announced his confession.

You can pick up the story in Matthew 16, where Jesus inquired of Peter and the disciples, "Who do you say I am?" (verse 15). I like to think it got quiet, like one of those awkward moments where people have something to say but don't feel comfortable saying it. While all the disciples suspected it, Peter, with his simple Galilean courage said it. "You are the Christ, the Son of the Living God." And even more astonishing than Peter's courage is what Christ said in response to Peter's confession: "Jesus replied, 'Blessed are you, Simon son of Jonah, for this was not revealed to you by man, but by my Father in heaven. And I tell you that you are Peter, and on this rock I will build my church, and the gates of Hades will not overcome it' " (Matthew 16:17, 18).

Because the Christian church has argued over these words for two thousand years, I'm confident that spelling out their various meanings will have to come at another time. But I want to draw your attention first to Peter and his journey from ignorance to understanding, and second to Christ's vision for a community of faith.

Between ignorance and understanding

When Peter makes his confession, what does he really believe? What does he really know? What does it mean that Jesus is the Christ (or the Messiah), the Son of the Living God? For Peter, it is likely that his view of Jesus at this pivotal stage is relatively ignorant. I don't think Peter gets it entirely. Here's why: although Peter courageously announces what many might suspect, his behavior from this point on screams the opposite.

1. He doesn't get Jesus' ultimate purpose. Not long after this declaration, Jesus describes His death in Jerusalem: "He then began to teach them that the Son of Man must suffer many things and be rejected by the elders, chief priests and teachers of the law, and that he must be killed and after three days rise again" (Mark 8:31). Peter cannot stomach the idea of the Messiah or the kingdom of God going down like that. He rebukes Jesus for talking about dying. Peter keenly demonstrates devotion, but still doesn't get the Savior's purpose.

Even today, ask members of any church to say in ten words or less who Christ is, and the range of answers will be significant. Moreover, ask church members to describe the mission of the church today, and you will find even more diversity of thought. Some will claim that we need to be about grace, good deeds, activism, truth, beauty, missions, and obedience to God's commands. But the kingdom God was revealing in Christ was still unfolding for Peter. The purpose of Christ may have been clear in Peter's mind (as it is in the minds of believers today), but this turned out to be quite cloudy in his understanding of what it should look like.

2. Peter doesn't get how duplicitous his own heart is. When Jesus warns Peter that this night Peter will deny him three times, Peter claims, "I will never deny you. I will die for you." No husband or wife on their wedding day believe they are capable of infidelity, but the well of selfishness in the human heart runs deep. You may have seen people testing the depth of a well by tossing a stone and listening for a splash. You measure the time it takes to hear the *kerplunk* and only imagine the depth. It is likely that we, like Peter, have a hard time imagining how deep our capacity is for faithlessness.

However, part of our humanness includes the unimaginable greatness we can achieve. We are created in God's image to aspire to that which is truly great—selflessness. It is in us. And anyone who been burned at the stake or tossed to the lions for God's sake probably never imagined faithfulness to God would require them to give so much. In that moment, Peter had no idea what he was capable of or what his loyalty would cost.

3. Peter doesn't fully get the mission of the church. Peter, full of the Holy Spirit at Pentecost, did not understand what it meant to be the church. He still held tightly to his rigid categories of what it meant to be an insider and an outsider. How long did it take Peter to get the truth that this grace, of which he had so deeply drunk, was as free to the Gentiles as it was for him? Well, more than ten years later, in the development of the New Testament church, Peter had a moment where Paul called Peter out publicly over Peter's inability to stand up to the narrow-minded pressure of the Jewish mission. Paul writes, "When Peter came to Antioch, I opposed him to his face, because he was clearly in the wrong. Before certain men came from James, he used to eat with the Gentiles. But when they arrived, he began to draw back and separate himself from the Gentiles because he was afraid of those who belonged to the circumcision group" (Galatians 2:11, 12). So here is Peter, after the birth and boom of the church, still struggling to understand the scope and meaning of the gospel message and the work of the church.

Nevertheless, although Peter did not fully know, he believed. He did not completely understand this thing called church—but he embraced it. Jesus embraced Peter's short-sighted and shallow faith for what it truly was—a start. Christ honored Peter by saying, "God revealed this to you Peter, when people confess Me to the world, nothing, not even the gates of hell will overcome it." It begins the same way with you and me. A start. A flicker of understanding mixed with some misunderstanding. A glimpse, but not the full, vivid picture. Like Peter, you may know only part of the story of our eternal home, but it is enough to start walking.

Why is this an important moment? This is the first time Jesus mentions the church. Church begins with Peter, short on all the information—but having enough inspiration to say, "Jesus, You are the One we have been waiting for. The Son of God. The Savior of the world."

So two thousand years later, here we are. And church begins with what we say about who Christ is and what He has done for us. Even if our data is somewhat skewed or our emphasis is off a bit, as a community of people, we start together toward home. Stop and take a moment to thank God for walking you home, just as you are.

The choice

So the walk home requires a choice—a decision—a public statement of what you value. It is expensive but worth it. Don't let the cost of starting your walk home distract you from its ultimate value. Part of our problem today is that we look at the price tag instead of at the value.

In Matthew 13:44–47, Jesus compared following Him to such a

choice about value: "The kingdom of heaven is like a treasure hidden in the field, which a man found and hid again; and from joy over it he goes and sells all that he has and buys that field. Again, the kingdom of heaven is like a merchant seeking fine pearls, and upon finding one pearl of great value, he went and sold all that he has and bought it" (NASB).

Maybe we have found *the* guiding question, stated several ways, for those who want to make their way home. What is your hidden treasure? What is your pearl of great price? What matters most to you? What do you treasure more than anything else? What are you willing to do or give to gain your greatest desire? What treasures do you cling to that you may have to surrender?

We stand at the start of the trailhead. We stand, although we are well aware of what sin has done and how it works in our hearts. We can stand, because we stand on the promise that God in Christ has redeemed us. The question surfaces, Do we love Jesus Christ and the hope of heaven more than anything else? The answer is—We want to.

At this point, we begin to become *belovers*. Leonard Sweet captured the concept of beloving by unpacking the etymology of the word *believe*: "The word *believe* is an ancient compounding of the verb *be* and the noun *life*. To 'believe' is to 'be-live'—to live your being, to trust your 'being' to 'life.' To give my heart to or to hold dear. . . . Philosopher William Cantwell Smith suggests that the German word for belief (*be-lieben*) comes closest to conveying the word's true meaning. The adjective *lieb* means 'dear' or 'beloved.' . . . Smith's definition of belief as 'beloved' comes closest to bringing us to the deeply relational context of the Hebrew idea of 'believer.' "[1]

To believe is to belove. According to the Hebrew mind, believing and receiving are inseparable. But in the West, we have tried to keep the ideas distinct. Perhaps the most deadly blow crippling the Christian church is the bifurcation of belief and experience. But even during the time the New Testament was written, the Greek mind split the world of ideas and reality into two separate realms. Perhaps this is why James downplays the contemporary notions of dividing thought and action, saying, "You believe that there is one God. Good! Even the demons believe that—and shudder" (James 2:19). Essentially he is saying, "You may believe (think or know), but even Satan knows the truth about Jesus. But it's not enough to know what is true, we must belove the One who is the Truth."

Believing and receiving, like learning to ride a bike, is an acquired skill. At first, there is no intuition other than self-preservation—don't fall! But as we practice, we get the feel of some aspects of riding: balance, multitasking between steering, pedaling, stopping, and praying. (This is my experience. I became very religious while learning how to ride a bike.) All of this comes only from acting on our desire to learn. Every new action is awkward, but with intentional practice, our action becomes an intuitive response—or what we call "second nature." In the Gospel of John, we notice how people move to activate their walk with Jesus: "Yet to all who *received* him, to those who *believed* in his name, he gave the right to become children of God—children born not of natural descent, nor of human decision or a husband's will, but born of God" (John 1:12, 13; emphasis added).

Clearly the two inseparable realities that emerge as we start our journey are believing and receiving. Both stir up thought and require action. They are the teeter-totter of our conversion experience.

I first experienced beloving after graduating from high school. I left home, went away to college, found a job, and began living my life as an independent adult. I don't ever remember making a decided choice to disengage from God or the community of faith, but I did choose to do so, little by little. Maybe one of sin's tricks is the subtle deception of small regression. I never said to God or about God, "I don't believe in You, nor do I want to follow You." But with every new day, I became more skilled at stiff-arming God's voice in my life until a callous grew over my heart. I lost contact with God, contact with family, and contact with my senses. While I was not engaged in substance abuse or anything illegal, I stopped going home. Instead of being dialed in and headed toward heaven, I simply began to wander.

The difference between a walk home and wandering is too perfect an example from my experience. The walk home has a beginning, there is a stride and a purpose, and there is a destination. Wandering? Well, you take a step, and it is usually the easiest step, and you simply follow one mindless movement with another. No purpose. No destination. No meaning, but always moving.

I woke from my wandering when my father traveled a couple hours on Saturday morning to "find me." He was worried about me. Sitting at a table having lunch, he reminded me of home. He said, "Troy, you are my son, and there is nothing you will ever do that will change that." I think he repeated his words then ended with an invitation: "Troy, come home." Home is where I remember being alive. Home is where I first felt a sense of purpose. Home was not only a house with a mom and dad and brothers, but it was a journey. Home is where my story began. As a family, we had decided to go on a walk destined for heaven—but somewhere along the way I got lost. But here is the point: I felt conviction. I saw my sin for what it was. I knew what I should do. I wanted to go home. I began to "believe" when I chose to quit my wandering and come home. Quitting my job, packing up my apartment, telling my friends, explaining the entire process became my confession. And with every decision I made, my feet found solid ground. It was like riding a bike.

When John says, "Everyone who believes and receives Christ is given the right to become children of God," he describes the rebirth experience, which makes us heirs—inheritors of an eternal home. He describes the starting point for those who make their way home.

Imagine how Peter and everyone else in Jerusalem and in the Judean countryside felt when John came calling them all to repentance. John's message did not just start a revival of complacent churchgoers; his preaching caused a revolution: "And so John came, baptizing in the desert region and preaching a baptism of repentance for the forgiveness of sins. The whole Judean countryside and all the people of Jerusalem went out to him. Confessing their sins, they were baptized by him in the Jordan River" (Mark 1:4, 5).

Repentance would be expected, but not baptism. Baptism was for non-Jews who wanted to convert. Their baptism marked their entrance into the family of Abraham. So when John called the Jews to repent, confess, and be baptized, it began a revolution. What might this look like today? Imagine every Christian church in the country sending out a mass e-mail to all who claim to be Christian, saying, "We can no longer be Christians in name only. If you want to be a Christian, think about what it means to be a follower of Christ, come to church this week, and sign up for membership in the faith. You will get an ID card that demonstrates your confession. Thanks. Hope to see you there. Sincerely, J. T. B."

How would you react to such a note? Many would be insulted. Some would leave. Some would claim, "I don't need anyone to authenticate my faith." But many would come to church and confess their love and loyalty to Christ, because nothing matters more than walking home with Jesus. I'm not in any sense saying this is a good idea, but I compare it to John, who basically excommunicated the Jews who thought they were saved by their Jewishness and charged them to repent and come in by faith. The amazing part of the story as told by Mark is this: "[They] went out to him. Confessing their sins, they were baptized." In essence, John called the people to become born again, by faith in the deliverance to come, not by birthright or bloodline.

The people made their confession through the act of baptism. While the meaning of baptism has taken many twists and turns throughout the centuries, a few truths continue to ring clear in its practice today. The Bible conveys at least three themes that are tied to baptism: adoption, forgiveness, and community.

Adoption

Upon hearing the salient truth from the mouth of Christ, "You must be born again," Nicodemus wondered, "How can a person be born again?" And the response of Jesus came quickly: "By water and the Spirit." Before baptism can represent the "death, burial, and resurrection of Christ," we must first understand what *that* has to do with us. John 1:12, 13 claim, "To all who received him, to those who believed in his name, he gave the right to become children of God—children born not of natural descent, nor of human decision or a husband's will, but born of God." Baptism is first relational.

Immediately after Christ went under the water in the Jordan and came up, a Voice from heaven said, "You are my Son, whom I love; with you I am well pleased" (Mark 1:11). Did Jesus need to hear these words? Did He experience some sort of identity crisis in which He did not know who He was? I know humanity has. While God views all humanity as His children, He will not force us into His family, so He extends the invitation to be born again by faith. In baptism, we clear up our identity crisis and confess to whom we belong. Naturally, by birth or adoption, we become part of a family—related to someone. In a similar way, we enter into a formal relationship to God through confessing our commitment to Christ in baptism.

Consider this parable: A teenage girl (we'll call her Susan) once became so filled with anger against her parents that she decided to run away from her home. She scribbled her hatred toward them on a note she left on the breakfast table. "This is my certificate of divorce. You are no longer my parents. I am no longer your daughter. I'm gone." She left before dawn.

Normally when young people run away, they go around the block, get hungry, forget their anger, and return home. Not Susan. She was long gone by the time her parents awoke and found the note. She hitchhiked her way across the state and into another part of the country. Finally, she felt free. Meanwhile, her parents and authorities searched frantically for her. The local police, sheriff's office, and the FBI were all looking for Susan, but she could not be found.

One morning the phone rang and a deep voice on the other line said, "We think we found your daughter. She is alive, but got caught up in a prostitution ring. She lives in a state where a person age seventeen is considered an adult, so we can't force her to return home to you, unless she indicates she wants to come home. Would you like to send her a message?" The mother replied, "Yes, tell her we love her and just want her to come home."

The authorities gave Susan the message. When all the good memories flooded back and she contrasted them to her now empty life, Susan decided to return home. Needless to say, her parents welcomed her back with joy. Her room had not changed. The same pictures were on the walls. For weeks she tried to settle in, but something still was not right. The relationship was awkward. Although her parents never brought up the circumstances of her leaving, she could not forget what she had written.

One morning she came downstairs and placed a piece of paper on the same breakfast table before her parents. On the top of the page were the words "Certificate of Adoption." She had drawn up an agreement for adoption with a place for her and her parents to sign. Confused, her mother said, "Susan, I can't sign this. You are my daughter. We have always been your parents. We didn't sign your divorce papers, and we don't need to sign this. You belong to us, as you always have."

Susan put her arms around her parents as tears came running down her cheeks, "I know how you feel about me. This certificate is not for your benefit, but for mine. I chose to leave, and this is my way of choosing you back. I need to say this. Please, let me let you adopt me." They understood and signed.

From God's point of view, there has never been a moment when you were not His child. But because of our sin, we face the truth that we must be born again—adopted back into the family. When we are baptized, we are signing the adoption papers. Paul said, "Praise be to the God and Father of our Lord Jesus Christ, who has blessed us in the heavenly realms with every spiritual blessing in Christ. For he chose us in him before the creation of the world to be holy and blameless in his sight. In love he predestined us to be adopted as his sons through Jesus Christ, in accordance with his pleasure and will—to the praise of his glorious grace, which he has freely given us in the One he loves" (Ephesians 1:3–6).

When we choose to go into the water, we are baptized into the name of Jesus Christ—into His family. Again, in Galatians, the apostle states, "You are all sons of God through faith in Christ Jesus, for all of you who were baptized into Christ have clothed yourselves with Christ" (Galatians 3:26, 27). As a result, we get to claim His name, His family, His home, and His cause in the world.

Forgiveness

Peter also includes the idea that baptism brings about "the forgiveness of sins." When Peter spoke to the small crowd on the Day of Pentecost, the words he spoke cut to the listeners' hearts. They wanted to know, What do we do now? Peter replied,

> "Let all Israel be assured of this: God has made this Jesus, whom you crucified, both Lord and Christ." When the people heard this, they were cut to the heart and said to Peter and the other apostles, "Brothers, what shall we do?" Peter replied, "Repent and be baptized, every one of you, in the name of Jesus Christ for the forgiveness of your sins. And you will receive the gift of the Holy Spirit. The promise is for you and your children and for all who are far off—for all whom the Lord our God will call" (Acts 2:36–39).

Baptism is the way God calls us to confess His sacrifice for us at Calvary. Paul captures the significance of baptism as it relates to the cross. "Don't you know that all of us who were baptized into Christ Jesus were baptized into his death? We were therefore buried with him through baptism into death in order that, just as Christ was raised from the dead through the glory of the Father, we too may live a new life" (Romans 6:3, 4).

If "all have sinned and fallen short of the glory of God" and the "wages of sin is death," someone has to pay. We have one of two choices: we can pay ourselves or we can let Christ redeem us. In baptism, we formally and publicly choose to let Christ pay. But Romans 6 claims that if we choose to let Christ pay with His life, we, too, are raised to life because of His resurrection. In essence, with baptism, we go through the entire experience: from death to life.

The importance of publicly testifying to this choice should not be understated. If we are asking God to wash away our sins in baptism, we also invite Him to cover our Sin. Our sins are the deeds, misdeeds, and even missed deeds we failed to do. But sins are the symptom of the problem of Sin. Claiming Christ's death and resurrection addresses both the Sin and the sins. Christ says, "Everyone who confesses Me before men, I will also confess him before My Father" (Matthew 10:32, NASB). Essentially, baptism—our public confession of Christ—declares to the world that God is paying for our entrance home.

Community

The rite of baptism throughout the Bible in inextricably tied to participation in a community of faith. The people, as a result of their mutual confession, gathered, worked, shared, and learned together what it meant to be a disciple. The word *community* basically means "sharing things in common with others." *Fellowship* is another word used to describe this experience in the life of the church. Take a peek at what it looks like in action:

> They devoted themselves to the apostles' teaching and to the fellowship, to the breaking of bread and to prayer. Everyone was filled with awe, and many wonders and miraculous signs were

done by the apostles. All the believers were together and had everything in common. Selling their possessions and goods, they gave to anyone as he had need. Every day they continued to meet together in the temple courts. They broke bread in their homes and ate together with glad and sincere hearts, praising God and enjoying the favor of all the people. And the Lord added to their number daily those who were being saved (Acts 2:42–47).

Some people fall in love with Christ but have bad experiences with Christians, so they try to receive Christ but reject one of His basic teachings: a community of faith. I know I'll get in trouble for saying this, but you cannot give your life completely to Christ and utterly forsake the community He established. I love the book title *When Bad Christians Happen to Good People* because it articulates how crucial the community of faith is. The entire Christian movement is set to rise or fall on the fellowship of believers. Paul links baptism to fellowship in the church, saying, "The body is a unit, though it is made up of many parts; and though all its parts are many, they form one body. So it is with Christ. For we were all baptized by one Spirit into one body—whether Jews or Greeks, slave or free—and we were all given the one Spirit to drink" (1 Corinthians 12:12, 13). To suggest that you are becoming a disciple of Christ but not a part of the church is to deny the very desire of Christ. Read Christ's prayer in John 17 and consider the impossibility of accepting Christ and not His family. To try to do so is to *except* Christ, not accept Him.

When I look at the huge task that stands before the church, I'm perplexed. God knows, and so do we, that the church has done both great good and has inflicted pain and caused serious damage. It is likely that anyone reading this book bears the scars from criticism, abuse, and prejudice—behavior unlike Christ's. I'm certain that you have been misunderstood, and I know that some of you have been ignored, dismissed, and even alienated by mean people. And if we all think long and hard, we might recall times when we have not behaved in a manner that would cause

Christ to smile. In addition is the damage we do without even knowing it. And if no one has said so to you before, I'll say it today: "I am sorry." "We were wrong." "That's not what our Savior taught us to do." On behalf of the church, I beg you to please forgive us for being cold, blind, and weak. It is likely that we are no better than Peter, a guy who can confess his belief and undying loyalty to Christ and a few hours later disown Him in a matter of moments or in a moment of weakness. Like Peter, we don't fully get it. But we will never improve at "getting it" apart from each other.

When Jesus said, "You are the salt of the earth," and "You are the light of the world," He used the plural form of *you.* "You, when you are together, are salt." "You, when you work together, are a light." Community is the framework of God's plan to spread the gospel to the world, and even though it is not perfect, there really is no other way.

We would do well to be mindful of people around the world who pay a heavy price for this treasure called the journey home. In parts of the world freedom reigns and certain blessings emerge from the abundance of choices. Yet in those places where freedom rings, so does apathy and weak-willed loyalties that fade at the first touch of adversity. But when the value of liberty is high because it comes at a high price, some have chosen to start the walk home. Consider the story of Meropi Gjika, who during the Communist regime of Albania, was forced to wait fifty years for her baptism.

Gjika learned about Christ under the radar of the Communist regime in the 1940s. Daniel Lewis [a missionary to Albania from the United States] studied and prayed with her, but was imprisoned by the Communist government. Gjika lived faithfully for forty-seven years without being able to meet with a larger community of believers. When Daniel Lewis had been imprisoned for his gospel work, she would often look after him in prison by sending him food and clothes. Gjika endured more than four decades of repression, but each week she would lay aside her tithes and offerings in hope that one day she would be able to openly join the body of believers without fear. In the 1990s when Communism fell, the hiding believers in Albania were able to worship openly, and

Gjika at the age of ninety-seven came to be baptized. What a day it was when she came up out of the water! What a day for her to hand the tithes and offerings to the church as an expression of her devotion and commitment to the community of faith!

"When I met Meropi for the first time in 1991, I was overwhelmed by the radiant faith and hope that she exuded," said Ray Dabrowski, communication director for the Adventist Church at that time. "I could not believe that against all odds, in a country that prohibited religion, she would continue and save her tithe money hoping that one day she would give it to the Lord."

Gjika said she had three dreams. "The first one was to be baptized. The second dream was to hand over [her] tithe and offerings to the church. And now, [she was] waiting to see a church built here." Gjika's first two dreams were fulfilled. But she died at the age of ninety-seven still hoping, still enduring. And now her third dream is fulfilled, a church exists in Tirana, Albania. The believers in Tirana are probably not perfect, but my guess is that they will become like Christ as they continue their walk home—together.[2]

Becoming a belover prompts a confession—a tangible expression of your decision to make your way home. You can't come to this place without a sense of your own sin and a deep appreciation for God's generous mercy. As hard as it may be to believe this new life is available by resting on the promise Christ gave, it becomes even harder to see why anyone would refuse such a gift. Nonetheless, for those who bank on the promises of God and confess their trust in Him, everything changes on the way home.

---

1. Leonard Sweet, *Out of the Question . . . Into the Mystery* (Colorado Springs, Colo.: WaterBrook Press, 2004), 27.
2. Bettina Krause, "Albania: A Woman of 'Great Faith and Obedience' Dies," *Adventist News Network*, February 20, 2001, http://news.adventist.org/2001/02/albaia-a-woma-of-great-faith-a-obeiece-ies.html (accessed November 4, 2009).

Questions for Reflection

1. Think about a time when you were lost and all you wanted was to be home? What was it like to finally arrive? What happened when you were found or came to the realization that you were, in fact, going home? How is this experience like making our way home to heaven?

2. To what degree are we driven by rewards? Do you think that it is possible to do anything good without a sense of what the reward would be?

3. In this chapter, two men came asking similar questions about the reward of eternal life: a young ruler and a teacher of the law (Luke 10:25–37 and Mark 10:17–31). How are these two individuals the same and how are they different?

4. This chapter describes Peter's journey as a work in progress. It shows how Peter's ideas, motives, and commitments changed as he followed Christ. To what degree do our motives change with our experience? Do we learn to love Christ before we make our way home or as we make our way home?

5. What are some truths in the Christian faith that people believe but may not really "belove"? How is this true for you? As you make your way home, what about this journey are you learning to "belove"?

6. This chapter describes baptism from three different vantage points: adoption, forgiveness, and community. Which of these three seems to be emphasized most in your experience? Which do you wish were emphasized more? Why?

7. This first section focused on how we take our first steps on the way home. Before you move on to the next section, pause and take a moment to pray and thank God for providing you with the way home and the promises to help you along the way.

Part 2: Stride Home

Many have an idea that they must do some part of the work alone. They have trusted in Christ for the forgiveness of sin, but now they seek by their own efforts to live aright. But every such effort must fail. Jesus says, "Without Me ye can do nothing." Our growth in grace, our joy, our usefulness,—all depend upon our union with Christ. It is by communion with Him, daily, hourly,—by abiding in Him,—that we are to grow in grace. He is not only the Author, but the Finisher of our faith. It is Christ first and last and always. He is to be with us, not only at the beginning and the end of our course, but at every step of the way. David says, "I have set the Lord always before me: because He is at my right hand, I shall not be moved." Psalm 16:8.

Do you ask, "How am I to abide in Christ?" In the same way as you received Him at first. "As ye have therefore received Christ Jesus the Lord, so walk ye in Him." "The just shall live by faith." Colossians 2:6; Hebrews 10:38. You gave yourself to God, to be His wholly, to serve and obey Him, and you took Christ as your Saviour. You could not yourself atone for your sins or change your heart; but having given yourself to God, you believe that He for Christ's sake did all this for you. By faith you became Christ's, and by faith you are to grow up in Him—by giving and taking. You are to give all,—your heart, your will, your service,—give yourself to Him to obey all His requirements; and you must take all,—Christ, the fullness of all blessing, to abide in your heart, to be your strength, your righteousness, your everlasting helper,— to give you power to obey.[1]

The Christian walk home has a certain stride. A stride is a "walk with long regular steps, often briskly or energetically."[2] This is what Peter had in mind when he urged, "For this very reason, make every effort to add to your faith goodness; and to goodness, knowledge; and to knowledge, self-control; and to self-control, perseverance; and to perseverance, godliness; and to godliness, brotherly kindness; and to brotherly kindness, love" (2 Peter 1:5–8).

One word, one phrase can make a significant difference in meaning. From deep within old files in my office I found a list of mistakes made on medical charts in which one word or phrase made a difference—a big difference in the interpretation.

- The patient refused autopsy.
- Patient has left white blood cells at another hospital.
- Patient has chest pain if she lies on her left side for over a year.
- On the second day, the knee was better, and on the third day it disappeared.
- The patient has been depressed since she began seeing me in 1993.
- She is numb from her toes down.
- The skin was moist and dry.
- Occasional, constant, infrequent headaches.
- Patient was alert and unresponsive.
- Rectal examination revealed a normal size thyroid.

- I saw your patient today, who is still under our car for physical therapy.
- The lab test indicated abnormal lover function.
- Skin: Somewhat pale but present.
- Patient has two teenage children, but no other abnormalities.

It is likely that many have misunderstood the nature of our work in the walk toward home. Notice how Peter switches gears and seemingly contradicts himself when, after having said, "Salvation is God's gift to us," he states, "For this very reason, make every effort." But note the first phrase, "For this very reason" (2 Peter 1:5).

"In view of all this" (NLT).
"Now for this very reason" (NASB).
"Because you have these blessings" (NCV).
"And beside this" (KJV).

One short phrase makes a difference. Every translator notes the distinction that we often fail to realize in our walk with Christ. When Christ saved us at Calvary, He made us safe. Free. And this reality may be new to us, but many of us have stumbled in the stride and even given up because we feel we have been given a gift and we must not ruin it with our bad behavior. Or, we reason, God's grace is a gift but we have to maintain it. All of these slivers of thought cause a cosmic diversion over the course of the walk. It's like having a car with badly aligned tires—over time the car will veer off the road instead of remaining straight and true. We will ultimately despair if we try to maintain something we could never achieve on our own. If we aren't good enough to earn our salvation, we surely aren't good enough to maintain it. It's simply wrongheaded to think we can.

But don't mistake the capacity to live fully for God's purposes with the ability to save yourself from your sin. We have settled that. All have sinned. All need a Savior. What we do have is the will to want to be like Christ—which is what begins to happen to us on the walk home. And even though we have a propensity to be selfish, rebellious—sinful, we also are compelled to good works by the very DNA in our humanness— not the humanity that says, "I'm only human," but the humanness that is imprinted with the nobility of our Creator, which claims, I am created in His image. When you see someone mistreating a child, where do you think the anger comes from? When you see a beautiful act of mercy, why does your heart sing? It is in your DNA. Again, it is tainted, weak, and untrained, but the capacity to grow into Christ's likeness is within each precious child of God.

So please! Don't make the mistake or mistake my words. Remember that whatever we work at, we are adding lavishly to faith! Faith in the promises God has made about our eternal home and how we can receive grace by faith. We don't add to God's grace but we strive to experience and flesh it out in our characters.

Paul would agree with Peter: "Therefore, my dear friends, as you have always obeyed—not only in my presence, but now much more in my absence—continue to work out your salvation with fear and trembling, for it is God who works in you to will and to act according to his good purpose" (Philippians 2:12, 13). Flesh it out. Experience the effects of grace working in your life. Live a life of praise to God for what He has already promised you.

The one little phrase "for this very reason" reveals the motivation for our "whollyness." Without a "because of this," we would chase our tails in futile legalistic pursuit, trying to achieve our eternal home, desperately hoping to catch what is already ours. This section is about how we grow on the walk. We will discover that training is different from trying. Striding is not striving. Learning is not earning. The change that we all long to experience requires effort, but the purpose of that effort is not to merit or maintain salvation, but to practice the virtues of grace with all our might. In other words, be wholly. Wholly give yourself to the journey of learning to be like Christ. Guilt free, because you are born of God by His grace and power, you can work out your salvation because it is yours, and you want to take it for a ride.

And in the same way you learn anything, you will fail. You will struggle. Your learning will expose your weaknesses. You will need to study, learn, reflect, wonder, listen, calculate, practice, experiment, and persist. Peter is not talking about simply giving good works a try; rather, he is calling for us to spend all we have to experience these qualities. The history of the next phrase in this passage is powerful: "make every effort to add . . ." (2 Peter 1:5). In ancient Greece, plays were great spectacles but required enormous choirs for impact. The word Peter uses is *epichoregein,* or to equip, which is the same idea used for assembling a choir. But these choirs were not simply a gathering of singers; they were organized with a spare-no-expense approach. *To equip* meant to spend all you have if you must for the cause. No chintzy giving or halfhearted attempts.

William Barclay captures Peter's intent well: "Peter urges his people to equip their lives with every virtue, and that must not be simply equipping to a necessary minimum, but lavishly and generosity. The very word is an encouragement to be content with nothing less than the loveliest and the most splendid life."[3]

That splendid life is what we experience and learn as we walk home. The important distinction to make is that these qualities are the by-products that grow out of a full-effort cooperation with God.

> Peter listed seven characteristics of the godly life, but we must not think of them as seven beads on a string or even seven stages of development. The word translated "add" really means "to supply generously." In other words, we develop one quality as we exercise another quality. These graces relate to each other the way the branch relates to the trunk and the twigs to the branch. Like the "fruit of the Spirit" (Gal. 5:22-23), these qualities grow out

of life and out of a vital relationship with Jesus Christ. It is not enough for the Christian to "let go and let God," as though spiritual growth were God's work alone. Literally, Peter wrote, "Make every effort to bring alongside." The Father and the child must work together.[4]

So, the practitioner in me asks, "OK, how does this happen?" If goodness, knowledge, self-control, perseverance, godliness, kindness, and love are the by-products of something else, what produces these qualities? Christ is to become our "Rabbi." Jesus said, "Every one who is fully trained will be like his teacher" (Luke 6:40). More specifically, we engage in the exercises (or disciplines) of the spiritual life. The word *disciple* means "someone who is taught." And with all the theology-speak today about discipleship, the most respectful application of the term *discipleship* is a devotion to learn to become like Christ. For this endeavor we need the world of teaching and learning. And learning requires discipline without the fear of failure. Notice I didn't say the presence of failure, but the fear of failure. If I'm afraid to try because the result is life or death, I'm going to freeze up and hope for another way. If I'm aware that real learning is more about effort than an impeccable result, there is freedom to discover.

Take a look in any effective classroom full of kindergarten students, and you will find a teacher who creates a positive atmosphere and attitude for learning. Peter is the perfect one to preach this because he is the poster boy for learning through experience. Experience is our most effective classroom. Experientially, we know there is a huge difference between teaching and telling. And we also know that learning is not some magical, immediate event, but an enduring process of transformation over time.

While I was developing a series of devotionals, I went online to purchase some visual aids from the Chas. C. Hart Seed Company. I scanned the Web site hoping to acquire actual mustard seeds to illustrate a talk on faith. I read what the pros in seed growing wrote about the time of growth for the mustard seed. I kid you not. The description read, "40 days to maturity." Forty days isn't a magic number, but throughout Scripture it becomes a symbol for the amount of time it takes for change to occur.

- After His baptism, Jesus spent forty days in the wilderness.
- God sent forty days of rain to flood the earth.
- Both times Moses received the commandments from God, he was on the mountain forty days.
- Elijah spent forty days of searching and struggling after the event on Mount Carmel.
- In the book of Jonah, God gave the people of Nineveh forty days to change their ways.
- After His resurrection, Jesus spent forty days with His disciples before ascending into heaven.

I don't know a whole lot about the biblical use of the number forty, but I do know that learning, transformation, and growth take time and exercise. So with each chapter in this section, I will suggest a few exercises that will call for your effort. Over time you will see your confidence grow as you make your way home.

Remember that fruit-bearing disciples are not super saints, but they live wholly bent toward heaven in a deliberate walk with God. Their growth is the result of divine grace in their hearts and minds. Their lifestyle is marked by the exercises that strengthen the muscles of their soul, and their souls are marked by the presence of the Holy Spirit. If there is one reality that is clear about the walk home, it is this: no one accidentally stumbles toward Christlikeness or has the way made easier for him by waiting for a more convenient set of circumstances.

"Make every effort to add," is not a contribution to your salvation or adding to what Christ has already done for you. There is nothing else you can do to secure grace or try to maintain what Christ has done for you at Calvary. To add to His perfect work is to suggest His work was not enough. No, by no means! *To add* means, "to implement." Flesh out today the qualities we love about our Lord. When we experience what it feels like to wear the character of the One we belong to, it will become a more natural fit. So, stride home as God works a work of transformation in you. This change is not your reward. The destination is your reward, and the challenge to "make every effort" is a call to engage in practices that will orient you to your new home.

1. Ellen G. White, *Steps to Christ*, 69, 70.

2. *Encarta World English Dictionary*, 1999, s.v. "stride."

3. William Barclay, *The Letters of James and Peter*, The Daily Study Bible series (Louisville, Ky.: Westminster John Knox Press, 1976), 299.

4. Warren Wiersbe, *Ephesians–Revelation*, vol. 2, The Bible Exposition Commentary New Testament (n.p.: Cook Communication Ministries, Chariot Victor Publishing, 1989), 438.

CHAPTER 5

Just Add Goodness

"Because of this, add to your faith, goodness."

Peter challenges those of us who have started the walk home to add to our faith—goodness. W. H. Auden once said, "Goodness is easier to recognize than define."

The Greek word for goodness is *arête,* which means "excellence" or "virtue" of an extraordinary quality. It is a desire to do the maximum possible effort for the noblest reason. In *Accept No Mediocre Life,* David Foster illustrates excellence with the example of Jan Ullrich and Lance Armstrong:

> The 1997 German winner, Jan Ullrich, was pursuing Lance Armstrong. In the thirteenth stage of the race, Ullrich had a bad crash. He was run off the road and thrown over his handlebars. Armstrong saw it, stopped, and waited while Ullrich recovered. Armstrong was ultimately victorious, and Ullrich took the runner-up trophy.
>
> Two years later in the 2003 Tour de France, as Armstrong sought a fifth consecutive victory, with Ullrich trailing him by a razor-thin 15 seconds, Armstrong hooked his handlebars on the bag of a fan leaning across the barrier. Ullrich stopped and waited while Armstrong picked himself up and remounted.[1]

There is no rule that says you must wait for a fallen competitor; it is a matter of honor. That is excellence! The apostle Paul would concur, saying, "Finally, brothers, whatever is true, whatever is noble, whatever is right, whatever is pure, whatever is lovely, whatever is admirable—if anything is excellent or praiseworthy—think about such things" (Philippians 4:8).

Clearly, we do not automatically add moral excellence to our lives. So, how does this work? How long does it take? How does excellence grow? From a practical perspective, where do we begin? Perhaps this change takes place from the outside in as well as from the inside out. Ask Demi-Lee Brennan.

In January 2008, a story made the rounds about a fifteen-year-old girl in Australia named Demi-Lee Brennan. She became the world's first known transplant patient to change blood types from O negative to O positive. How did this happen? She received a liver transplant, and the blood stem cells in Brennan's new liver invaded her body's bone marrow, slowly but steadily taking over her entire immune system. She now has an entirely different kind of blood. At first the doctors assumed someone had made a mistake, because it's always been assumed that a change like that can't happen.

The kind of change that Peter calls believers to go the extra mile for is similar to what happened to Demi-Lee Brennan. Yet goodness seems to be such an intrinsic virtue. When we say "he's a good man" or "she is such a good person," we characterize their essence as good. We imply that inside and out they are virtuous. So the doubt may easily creep in, *If we were born in sin, how can there be any good in us to take the first step from the trailhead?* Some might quickly reply, "It is Jesus who gives us the goodness, not anything in us." Be careful with that thought because if Jesus just hands us goodness, why does He give so much to some and so little to others? The metaphor Jesus used in John 15 to describe our transformation includes the idea of growing. "I am the vine; you are the branches. If a man remains in me and I in him, he will bear much fruit;

apart from me you can do nothing" (John 15:5).

We were born in sin, but we are also created in the image of God. We are created with the capacity to choose to obey or to go our own way. We are also created with the capacity to love unconditionally. Ask any parent—it's in there. Children are the perfect example of the transformation that takes place over time. They have an internal curiosity, a desire to know and to grow. But this desire for growth can be stifled. We can learn not to think, not to try, not to wonder, and never to dream. But look around a room full of children who are allowed and encouraged to know and grow—it's amazing, loud, and crazy—but amazing. So are we who start to walk, knowing that as we believe in the promise of Christ, we can give ourselves fully to excellence.

Also note that it might seem logical to think that the enemy of "goodness" is the opposite—badness or corruption. But if the word *goodness* means "moral excellence," there will be a relentless pursuit for the maximum instead of being content with mediocrity. Aristotle once said, "We do not act rightly because we have virtue or excellence, but we rather have those because we have acted rightly. We are what we repeatedly do. Excellence, then, is not an act, but a habit." The greatest danger to fostering the virtue of excellence is the acceptance of the notion of good enough.

God's goodness is a bedrock truth of Scripture. His goodness is praised in Psalms (25:8; 34:8; 86:5; 100:5; 118:1; 136:1; 145:9). Jesus affirms the Father's goodness when speaking to the rich young ruler (Matthew 19:17; Mark 10:18; Luke 18:19). In 1 Peter 2:3, Peter echoes the language of Psalm 34:8, "Taste and see that the LORD is good!"

Although we might discuss God's goodness in some abstract philosophical sense, in Scripture His goodness appears most clearly in His dealings with people. He is not only good in general, but He is good to us (Psalms 23:6; 68:10; 73:1; 119:65; 145:9; Lamentations 3:25; Luke 6:35; Romans 2:4; 11:22; Ephesians 2:7; Titus 3:4). Human goodness is modeled on divine goodness (Matthew 5:48). For human beings, goodness involves good behavior. Goodness expresses itself in kindness and includes avoiding evil.

It is nearly impossible to think about goodness in the abstract. In Scripture goodness always involves particular ways of behaving. Because God is good, He is good to His people; when people are good, they behave decently toward each other, based on God's goodness to them. Moses' invitation to Hobab expresses this concept: "Come with us and we will treat you well, for the LORD has promised good things to Israel" (Numbers 10:29).

Those who serve God will "seek good, not evil, . . . hate evil, love good" (Amos 5:14, 15).

God's appeal to His people to return to the covenant relationship finds expression in a call to simple goodness (Micah 6:6–8).

Les Parrott, in *Three Seconds,* tells the story of one person whose life of excellence manifested itself in going the extra mile:

> In August of 2002, the letter to the editor in *Newsweek* was a posthumous tribute to someone I had never heard of: Harry Quadracci, founder of Quad/Graphics, the largest privately owned printing company in the world. Back in 1977, Harry Quadracci was the owner of a small printing press in Wisconsin. Not usually a supplier to *Newsweek,* he took an urgent order when they were unable to get work done by their regular printer. They rushed him the layouts, but the plane they were on was diverted to Chicago by a snowstorm. When *Newsweek* staff found out, they called Quadracci in a panic. But they were surprised to find out that he had already sent a car to Chicago (in the blizzard) to retrieve the layouts, and they were by now on the press.[2]

Needless to say, *Newsweek* was impressed with the extra-mile approach that poured naturally out of Quadracci's way of doing business. The small town printer *had* anticipated the problem and *had* solved it before others even knew of the drama. A year later, *Newsweek* gave Quadracci all their Midwest business. There is an unmistakable goodness in those who go the extra mile.

God has modeled this kind of goodness toward us. In fact, the Bible describes God's goodness as *so good* that it is inexpressible, abundant, and lavished on all creation.

Peter, in his earlier letter to the saints who faced violent persecution, said to the believers, "Though you have not seen him, you love him; and even though you do not see him now, you believe in him and are filled with an *inexpressible* and glorious joy" (1 Peter 1:8; emphasis added).

Sometimes I wonder how much information we need in order to believe. These young believers had no New Testament, literature, inspirational videos, or anything other than the story of Jesus told by eyewitnesses. It seemed to be enough.

The beloved apostle John knew firsthand of the goodness of God. He recalled clearly all the times Jesus *had* referred to Himself in a way that captured who God was and what might cause us to believe more fully in Him. John penned the words Christ spoke, saying, "I am the gate; whoever enters through me will be saved. He will come in and go out, and find pasture. The thief comes only to steal and kill and destroy; I have come that they may have life, and have it to the full" (John 10:9, 10). Abundant. Overflowing. More than enough. Both John and Paul use the word *lavish* to describe God's goodness, which is not merely ample, but extravagantly good. John says, "How great is the love the Father has lavished on us, that we should be called children of God! And that is what we are!" (1 John 3:1). Paul echoes this theme when he writes to the Ephesians: "In him we have redemption through his blood, the forgiveness of sins, in accordance with the riches of God's grace that he lavished on us with all wisdom and understanding" (Ephesians 1:7, 8).

While waiting during another delay at the airport's departure gate, I stood staring at the counter where seemingly heartless agents proclaimed that we would have to rebook on another flight to get home. A man stood four feet from me and let out a sigh of disgust, "Oh good God. Not again." His words were more an expletive than a prayer. The woman on the other side of him chimed out, "Amen brother. God is good enough for me." I stiffen at these public encounters with Christians, the world, and quick conversations about God. They never seem to go well. But he immediately apologized, saying, "I'm sorry. I didn't mean to be offensive. I just have to get home and this always happens to me." She replied, smiling, "No apology necessary. It always happens to me, too, and I always come to the same conclusion when I get home—Good God."

He looked quizzically at her and offered, "I suppose so," and then he stepped forward to rebook his ticket home. I stood behind him in line as agents redirected the angry crowd one at a time. And because eavesdropping is one of my spiritual gifts, I listened carefully while praying, "Oh God, help this guy get home."

The ticket agent searched intently, checking all options, all airlines. The passenger sighed with audible relief when he heard the words, "I got you a seat on a flight that leaves in fifteen minutes. You'll have to make one stop, but you will arrive at your scheduled time."

"Yes!" I said quietly to myself. "What about first class, God? Can You be that good?" The agent added even before I finished my challenge, "Oh, by the way, I had to stick you in first class. Hope you don't mind." I'm aware that pastors are sometimes accused of embellishing stories— but this was one of those moments in which I was aware of God's immediate, attentive presence for days. God is good. I watched the happy man as he walked past the woman who had given him her eight-word testimony, and he slowed to say something, raised his ticket slightly as if to point upward, and made his way toward another gate. I couldn't hear what he said, but the woman wore a smile that seemed to be about ready to burst. Unfortunately, I did not have a similar experience with the agent. It took me hours to get home, but it was still good because I believed God was still good.

The goodness we are called to add to our faith grows within us as we practice the ways of our Father in heaven. Lavish. Abundant. Inexpressible. The extra mile. Practice a couple of exercises to strengthen the muscle of goodness in your heart. And remember, as we make our way home, we learn, not with perfect precision but with perfect trust in the good grace of God.

Practice secret kindness

One of the virtues of the discipline of secret kindness is that only God knows the good things you do. You remove the temptation to practice goodness to further a good reputation. There is an amazing joy of basking in God's smile as you lift up others. The key in practicing secret kindness is offering help that is abundant, even surprising. A friend once made a gift basket for a volunteer fireman in my community. She could have put in items that said, "Thank you," and it would have been received graciously. But she loaded the basket with gift cards and the finest foods, real dark chocolate, two tickets to a local play—she just overwhelmed him with excellent gifts. Such an excellent gift stirred the love of goodness in her heart and broke open a well of gratitude and grace in the one who received the gift.

Practice gratitude

In order to stride wholly to what is "most excellent," practice gratitude. Dietrich Bonhoeffer once said, "In ordinary life we hardly realize that we receive a great deal more than we give, and that it is only with gratitude that life becomes rich." It should also come as no surprise that gratitude comes from the same root as the word *grace*. Gratitude, in a beautiful, multifaceted way, stretches our capacity to imagine greatness. When we meditate and think of the great gifts with which we are blessed, we obtain experiential evidence of what is good, and we desire to do it. For what graces are you grateful? Make a list. Make a note. Send a text or an e-mail. Let the gratitude out so God's goodness in you can grow.

A young teacher illustrated how practicing "goodness" was like pouring water into a muddy cup. She placed a clear glass containing muddy water in the middle of a large basin and then began trickling clean water into the cup. The glass of mud slowly turned a slightly lighter shade of mud. Then the teacher began to pour the water with greater quantity, flushing the mud out. When the pitcher was empty, the clear glass was no longer filled with mud, but with fresh water. She lifted the glass and drank from it, saying, "If you want a little goodness in your life, you can trickle a few drops in here and there, but no real change will occur. Flood your life with goodness in such a way that there is no room for anything else, and the difference is clear." I thought the lesson was brilliant.

So ask yourself, what are the most excellent things that are available for you to do this week? Is there a character in Scripture that models this quality? Is there anyone you know who seems to demonstrate goodness that you might talk with and ask, "What activities give you the greatest joy from week to week?" Deepen your love for moral excellence by practicing it as you make your way home.

---

1. David Foster, *Accept No Mediocre Life: Living Beyond Labels, Libels, and Limitations* (Brentwood, Tenn.: Warner Faith, 2005), 33.

2. Les Parrott, *Three Seconds: The Power of Thinking Twice* (Grand Rapids, Mich.: Zondervan, 2007), 141.

Questions for Reflection

1. Who has been a shining example of goodness to you? What are some examples of how those people exhibited goodness to you?

2. How do you think goodness gets added to a person's faith? Is it modeled, practiced, desired, or just imparted?

3. What are some key examples of God's goodness in the Bible? If you could tell three stories that captured the goodness of God, what would they be?

4. How does the extra-mile principle shared in this chapter shape the way you think of the quality of goodness or moral excellence?

5. This chapter suggests that practicing secret acts of kindness and developing the habit of gratitude are ways to deepen the quality of goodness in believers. Choose one or both and invite a friend to join you in the exercise so that you can debrief and share the experience with each other.

6. How do you think that practicing the quality of goodness keeps us mindful about making our way home?

CHAPTER 6

Just Add Knowledge

"For this very reason, make every effort to add to your faith goodness; and to goodness, knowledge" (2 Peter 1:5).

"Those of you who think you know everything are very annoying to those of us who do" (Anonymous).

Knowledge for the sake of knowing can become a religion in itself. Do you know people who are fact junkies? Or perhaps you know people who love to know things that no one else really thinks much about. I subscribe to a magazine called *Mental Floss.* I so enjoy acquiring clever, useless information. The special presidential Fall 2008 issue contains a small column on bizarre presidential disabilities. William Howard Taft had a dented skull. James Madison had a deep scar on his nose from frostbite. Andrew Jackson apparently had a drooling problem, which supposedly worsened when he became angry. Benjamin Harrison wore gloves all the time to cover a serious rash on his hands. Thomas Jefferson had boils on his—well, Jefferson had boils. And James Buchanan was nearsighted in one eye and farsighted in the other. I suppose some of this stuff could be used in a quirky way, but honestly, the material is mostly useless.

Have you ever heard about dihydrogen monoxide? Be careful around this stuff. It's been around for a while, but it got a lot of media attention in 1997 when a fourteen-year-old student named Nathan Zohner circulated a petition to ban the substance as part of a high school science fair. According to Zohner, dihydrogen monoxide "may cause severe burns, accelerates the corrosion and rusting of many metals, and has been found in the excised tumors of terminal cancer patients." Despite these risks, he further noted, the nefarious chemical is often used "as an industrial solvent and coolant, in the production of Styrofoam, and as a fire retardant." It is a pretty impressive chemical that we know well—water.[1]

While I am not the *most* knowledgeable person I know, I do know stuff. For example I know that the word *queue* is the only word in the English language that is still pronounced the same way when the last four letters are removed. I know that beetles taste a little like apples, wasps taste like pine nuts, and worms (dried or fresh) have a baconlike flavor to them. I know that *almost* is the longest word in the English language with all the letters in alphabetical order.

Did you know that in 1386, the French executed a pig by public hanging for the crime of murder? I knew that. I know that a cockroach can live for several weeks with its head cut off! I also knew that Horatio Nelson, one of England's most illustrious admirals, never managed to find a cure for seasickness. As long as the ocean moved, his stomach heaved.

It has come to my attention that right-handed people live, on average, nine years longer than left-handed people. (However, as a left-hander, I'm certain that the 10 percent of us who are aliens on this planet live better, rather than longer.) I know that the elephant is the only mammal that can't jump. Fingernails grow four times faster than toenails. Women blink nearly twice as often as men. (I have a theory as to why: it is likely that men have something much more beautiful to look at than women and so our eyes are wide open, whereas women tend to shut their eyes to avoid what they have to look at. Just a theory.)

I know that some worms eat themselves if they can't find any food. I know that the longest recorded flight of a chicken is thirteen seconds, and a giraffe can actually clean its ears with its twenty-one-inch tongue. Nice.

I possess the knowledge that an ostrich's eye is bigger than its brain and that slugs have four noses. I know that the word *obdormition* is a technical term for the numbness when a part of your body goes to sleep. I hold in my mind the imperative knowledge about how a rat can last longer without food than a camel.

There is knowledge—and then there is stuff people know. None of the above facts are particularly helpful or necessary. Even if we are being totally serious about our knowledge, the nature of "knowing" today is much different from the knowledge Peter calls us to add to our faith. The biblical idea for knowledge has a wider sweep than our English word *know,* including perceiving, learning, understanding, willing, performing, and experiencing. *To know* is not to be intellectually informed about some abstract principle, but to apprehend and experience reality. Knowledge is not the possession of information, but rather its exercise or actualization.

Therefore, knowing God is not to know about Him in an abstract and impersonal manner, but rather to enter into His saving actions (Micah 6:5). To know God is not to struggle philosophically with His eternal essence, but rather to recognize and accept His claims. It is not solely some mystical contemplation, but includes dutiful obedience. In the doing of justice and righteousness, Josiah is said to have known God (Jeremiah 22:15, 16). True knowledge of God involves living according to His will, and the opposite of knowledge is not ignorance, but rebellion (verses 11–14).

Peter continues the list of virtues to which we should give ourselves wholly by adding knowledge to our goodness. The word used by Peter is *gnosis.* Gnosis is a practical knowledge—it is the ability to apply insight and experience to a particular situation. It is the knowledge that equips a person to make a good choice and to act honorably. Basically, this kind of knowledge is practical wisdom integrated into real life. One commentator adds about knowledge: "It refers to the ability to handle life successfully. It is the opposite of being 'so heavenly minded as to be of no earthly good!' This kind of knowledge does not come automatically. It comes from obedience to the will of God (John 7:17). In the Christian life, you must not separate the heart and the mind, character and knowledge."[2]

Peter would have seen this knowledge at work firsthand. In Mark 1, Jesus experiences a full Sabbath day: going to church, casting out a demon in between the personal ministries report and the opening hymn, going to Peter's home and healing his mother-in-law, only to find the entire town waiting at the door for healing as soon as the sun went down. The Bible says, "Very early in the morning, while it was still dark, Jesus got up, left the house and went off to a solitary place, where he prayed. Simon and his companions went to look for him, and when they found him, they exclaimed: 'Everyone is looking for you!' Jesus replied, 'Let us go somewhere else—to the nearby villages—so I can preach there also. That is why I have come' " (Mark 1:35–38).

Christ, exhausted by life's demands, finds clarity and courage to move on. To know what to do and when to do it epitomizes practical knowledge. The disciples and the townspeople might have looked at such a decision and come to a different conclusion, but Christ in solitude and prayer became clear about the next step.

Paul, having been trained under the finest thinkers, echoes a passion for this practical knowledge: "This is my prayer: that your love may abound more and more in knowledge and depth of insight, so that you may be able to discern what is best and may be pure and blameless until the day of Christ, filled with the fruit of righteousness that comes through Jesus Christ—to the glory and praise of God" (Philippians 1:9–11).

The knowledge spoken of by Peter, prayed for by Paul, and modeled by Christ is a useful, life-shaping insight into what is practical and effective. But remember, Adam and Eve fell partly because of their curiosity to know. God created us with the capacity and drive to learn, but even practical knowledge can be used for destructive purposes.

Parker Palmer teases apart the nuances of humanity's motivation for knowledge: "Adam and Eve were driven from the Garden because of the kind of knowledge they reached for—a knowledge that distrusted and excluded God. Their drive to know arose not from love but from curiosity and control, from the desire to possess powers belonging to God alone. They failed to honor the fact that God knew them first, knew them in their limits as well as their potentials. In their refusal to know as they were known, they reached for a kind of knowledge that always leads to death."[3]

Jesus charged the Pharisees with a misguided quest for knowledge, saying, "You diligently study the Scriptures because you think that by them you possess eternal life. These are the Scriptures that testify about me, yet you refuse to come to me to have life" (John 5:39, 40). If knowledge becomes the end in itself, then it ends in death. But knowledge can be a vehicle to understand and respond to the living Christ. Jesus said, "This is eternal life: that they may know you, the only true God, and Jesus Christ, whom you have sent" (John 17:3).

So, if we are to add to our goodness, knowledge, then we must begin with what we will choose to be our sources of knowing. Some lean completely on their own personal experiences. Others know what is true in life because they watch the news twenty-four hours a day. (And we all know the news media reports the truth—right?) We choose from whom or what we will get our information. What are your sources of knowledge? The Bible? Music? Friends? Teachers? Only what you see? Only what seems to work? Movies. Wikipedia. Blog content. Charismatic leaders. Art. Intuition. Science. The sources are endless, but as we make our way home, we must use our sources of knowledge wisely.

Perhaps the first and best source for knowledge is found in the pages of Scripture. It contains many punchy, short statements of wisdom and poignant phrases that attain universal popularity. The golden rule. Judge not, lest ye be judged. A stitch in time saves nine. Wait a minute, that may be sound knowledge, but that saying does not grow out of Scripture. And that illustrates the problem; we get solid sound bites, but no context or connection to the grand theme of life. Even more, the phrases of Scripture, if cut and pasted carelessly, can communicate a message God never had in mind. For example, when it comes to situations in life where honesty is costly, I could quote directly from the Bible, "A lie is an abomination to the Lord . . . and an ever present help in time of need." Under *that* kind of dubious methodology, anything can pass for knowledge. However, the Bible is much more than a book of magic phrases and heart-stabbing insights, and we know it, but I fear that today we are more familiar with the Bible than we are fed by it.

Taking a page out of Scripture

I glued the leather cover of a Bible over a cheap romance novel. The original Bible had been ruined by water damage in a flood, and only the cover was still intact. Why would I do this? To illustrate a point. While speaking to a youth group, I opened the pseudo-Bible I had made and began to tear pages irreverently and tossed them on the ground. The young people gasped. The parents glared and stood up, looking around for someone to remove me—clearly I was a heretic.

Immediately, I held up my hand and said, "Please know that I would never mistreat a Bible. This book is a fake and not a real Bible at all." The crowd looked somewhat relieved but still uncertain as to the point. I asked, "Why did you react the way you did when I tore the pages?"

"Because it is God's Word," and "It is a holy Book" came the responses from the still suspicious youth.

"I agree. The Bible is God's Word, and it is, without a doubt in my mind, holy." I said, trying to calm the defensive mob.

"But let me ask you, what is worse, tearing Bible pages out of disrespect—or completely ignoring it, knowing full well it is God's message to you?" So, which is more vile—hatred or indifference, distain or disregard, disrespect or disinterest? The ultimate lesson for me is that I have so much more knowledge about knowledge than I know what to do with, that it is easy to take God's Word for granted. Maybe it is time to embrace the knowledge of Scripture with a little more commitment and determination. Practicing the discipline of being informed and guided by God's Word doesn't make you perfect, but it does deepen your understanding of His will for your life as you make your way home.

Practice being guided by Scripture

The practice of searching the Scriptures to "find knowledge" is often fruitless, if not boring. Again, the type of knowledge Peter refers to is an active, practical application of information. Below are choice sentiments on gaining knowledge through God's revealed Word. Ellen White captures with simplicity and depth the discipline that adds knowledge to goodness.

> There is nothing more calculated to strengthen the intellect than the study of the Scriptures. No other book is so potent to elevate the thoughts, to give vigor to the faculties, as the broad, ennobling truths of the Bible. If God's word were studied as it should be, men would have a breadth of mind, a nobility of character, and a stability of purpose rarely seen in these times.
>
> But there is but little benefit derived from a hasty reading of the Scriptures. One may read the whole Bible through and yet fail to see its beauty or comprehend its deep and hidden meaning.[4]

OK, so how do we do it? It is likely that most people don't neglect Bible study because they don't believe the Bible as much as they avoid it because they don't know how or where to start. As you consider various methods of Bible study, you will notice that most devotional approaches are quite similar. You might start with one of the gospels or letters to the churches in Scripture. Even the Old Testament narratives are a rich place to begin. What is needed is a method that you continue to practice so that your eyes and mind can become more effective at seeing the knowledge that is right before your eyes. The following is a process that is helpful to me.

Step 1: Look at God's Word
Simply read the text carefully.

- With eyes that are open, observe the details in the text. The words, phrases, names, verbs, emotions, contrasts, lists, and conditions. Most of the work is detective business—looking for the pieces of the puzzle. You might try underlining, circling, highlighting specific things you notice, or drawing lines to connect ideas in a chapter.
- With eyes that imagine, picture the reality, the event, or the conversation with your sanctified imagination.
- With eyes that focus, ruminate on one idea, thought, or section at a time.

Step 2: Listen to God's Word
Try to hear the message God is saying to you in the passage.

- With ears to their world, listen so you can understand what the writer meant to say in his time and place.
- With the ears of your world, listen so you sense the relevance of God's Word to your world. The exercise is one of bridge-building and making meaningful connections!
- With ears to recognize the sound of God's voice speaking to your heart and life—listen personally.

Step 3: Learn from God's Word

Connect the message to the reality of your life, experience, and history.

- With a balanced mind to measure each passage in light of the whole of Scripture.
- With a practical mind to determine the areas of your life that need renewal and how that might occur.
- With a proactive mind that seeks to live differently in light of discovery.

Step 4: Live God's Word

Deliberately practice in a tangible way what you have discovered.

- With personal application that directly relates to your scenario and sphere of influence.
- With a pliable heart that is willing to be shaped by your study throughout the day.
- With a tangible response to God's Word. This is a specific response that you can know when you have done it. I can say, "I want to control my temper!" but a tangible application would be, "I'm going to control my temper in the basketball game tonight." The more specific the plan, the greater your chances are to remember to apply it.

Again, the work of learning how to do this is not magical, electric, or addictive. It takes a commitment and determination to become a student of the Scripture.

Practice being alone

Some might wonder how solitude fosters knowledge. But remember, earlier we referred to that busy day before which Jesus rose early in the morning to be alone and pray. The solitude offered Him the time and the stillness to gain some clarity about His mission. In our world, time and being still are at a premium. When you aren't used to being alone with God, you never feel at home in your own brain. Solitude creates space for God to get into you and for you to get into God. Think about the way a tea bag works. The longer the bag sits in the steaming water, the more the water gets deep into the bag of tea. As a result, what is in the bag gets into the water. It's not complicated to understand, but it's hard to practice.

Our frenzied lifestyle and constant camaraderie make us crazy and afraid of being alone and quiet. "Like rats on speed there seems to be a collective cultural influence on our lives that is powerful. What is missing? The individual. The self. People who are OK with being alone because they are not defined by culture, but by the living Christ. Look at Jesus dismissing the crowd, moving into the quietness of the mountains and being found alone—again. Jesus isn't shy, nor is He sick of ministry. He enters into moments of solitude to be mindful of who He is."

Ellen White urges believers to experience the possibilities of a reflective life when she states, "As we thus contemplate heavenly themes, our faith and love will grow stronger, and our prayers will be more and more acceptable to God, because they will be more and more mixed with faith and love. They will be intelligent and fervent. There will be more constant confidence in Jesus, and a daily, living experience in His power to save to the uttermost all that come unto God by Him."[5]

Those who practice reflective moments of solitude seem to have a strength of character that stands composed when the crowd is unraveling. Daniel. David. Esther. Elijah. Moses. John the Baptist. Jesus of Nazareth. Joseph. They all had to stop, think, reflect, and wonder in order to be the heroes they were in public. What did they know in the quiet place that enabled them to stand in the roar of trial? Give deliberate stillness a try and let your knowledge of God and His plan for you deepen.

Adding knowledge

The quest for knowledge runs deep in the human makeup, so much so that we often misuse the gift of knowledge and center our learning around ourselves. But looking at Christ, His Word, and the reality of life, we see with unmistakable clarity the purpose that our ability to know anything is for knowing our Creator. So many times Peter thought he knew. He knew what it meant for Christ to be the Messiah. He knew how many times to forgive, how Christ should talk, and what his own heart would do under pressure. But as Peter learned about living wholly for the Savior, he discovered that knowing Christ leads to a transformed life. The change that occurs as we make our way home is slight, but steady.

1. http://preachingtoday.com/illustrations/weekly/08-07-07/3070708.html.

2. Wiersbe, *Ephesians–Revelation*, 438.

3. Parker J. Palmer, *To Know as We Are Known: Education as a Spiritual Journey* (New York: HarperOne, 1993), 25.

4. White, *Steps to Christ*, 90.

5. *Steps to Christ*, 89.

Questions for Reflection

1. Why do you think Peter put knowledge after goodness in this list?

2. Think about the different kinds of knowledge we live with. If the knowledge Peter refers to is not the possession of information, but rather its exercise, then what do you know today? What are some experiences or reality-tested truths that you know, really know?

3. This chapter discusses the story of Christ missing sleep and going apart to pray as a way to add knowledge. When in your life have you found clarity and understanding in quiet moments alone with God?

4. A popular slogan states, "Knowledge is power." Do you agree with this statement? If so, why? If not, why not?

5. Read Philippians 1:9–11 and consider how love might grow "in knowledge and depth of insight." How might this be true in life? What are some examples that come to your mind?

6. Parker Palmer distinguishes between the different "kinds of knowledge" that tempted Adam and Eve in the Garden of Eden. How might this be true today? Examine your heart and ask, "What kind of knowledge do I crave? The knowledge that binds me to God or the knowledge that distinguishes me from God?"

7. One way to add knowledge is to allow Scripture to guide you through your life. Use the suggestions at the end of this chapter on a passage of Scripture and discover insights that may deepen your knowledge.

8. Another practice suggested to add knowledge is being alone or quiet. Without fail, your seasons of solitude will grow your understanding of yourself, God, and the world you live in. Choose a few pockets of time in your schedule this week during which to practice solitude. Consider writing down some of your thoughts about that experience for reflection.

CHAPTER 7

Just Add Self-Control

"For this very reason, make every effort to add to your faith goodness; and to goodness, knowledge; and to knowledge, self-control" (2 Peter 1:5, 6).

Justin John Boudin, a twenty-seven-year-old man from Minnesota, pled guilty to assault charges for losing his temper in a violent rage toward two people. Ironically, the perpetrator committed these crimes on his way to an anger-management class.

The police record reports that Boudin was waiting at a bus stop when he began to harass a fifty-nine-year-old woman. Apparently, he started yelling at her over what he felt was a lack of respect. The scene escalated, and the woman became frightened. When she tried to call the police on her cell phone, Justin Boudin punched her in the face. A sixty-three-year-old man jumped into the fray to try to defend the woman. Then Boudin started beating him on the back with a blue folder that contained all of his anger-management homework. In fact, the police were able to find Boudin by using the relevant data from the papers in the blue folder.[1]

It's not funny. (Well, maybe a little.) But it is ironic. It's true and unbelievable all at the same time. My first reaction to the story smacked of self-righteous pity and parental arrogance, but on further reflection, I wondered if a similar story could be found in my closet, and yours as well. If you don't struggle with self-control then good for you. At least be aware that you are capable of struggling with the inability to get a grip!

The word Peter uses is *egkrateia,* which literally describes the ability to take a grip of oneself. It does not mean a person completely suspends their desires, but rather, with full admission, chooses not to be swept away. Again, be mindful that these virtues are not links in a sequence or steps on the ladder of sanctification. Peter's challenge to add self-control to knowledge has to do with the way all of the attributes support and help believers walk home. Developing goodness deepens our capacity to know. Enriching your life with the quality of kindness enhances your capacity to love. Perhaps it is better to think of these virtues as concentric circles, rather than as a sequence. Either way you look at it, it takes making "every effort" to grow these qualities in your character.

Developing the muscle of the human will is and has always been a key feature of our stride as we make our way home. The first question we should ask is, What does Peter mean by *self-control*? And the next question that emerges with the practice of self-control is, If I'm not in control, who is?

Dr. Ben Carson has become famous throughout the world as a highly skilled pediatric neurosurgeon, but what some may not know is the struggle he had as a teenager with self-control. His temper almost redirected his steps in an entirely different path. In *Take the Risk,* Carson writes about the day he asked God to help him overcome his issue with self-control:

> One day, as a 14-year-old in ninth grade, I was hanging out at the house of my friend Bob, listening to his radio, when he suddenly leaned over and dialed the tuner to another station. I'd been enjoying the song playing on the first station, so I reached over and flipped it back. Bob switched stations again.
>
> A wave of rage welled up. Almost without thinking, I pulled

out the pocketknife I always carried and, in one continuous motion, flicked open the blade and lunged viciously right at my friend's stomach. Incredibly, the point of the knife struck Bob's large metal buckle and the blade snapped off in my hands.

Bob raised his eyes from the broken piece of metal in my hand to my face. He was too surprised to say anything. But I could read the terror in his eyes.

"I . . . I . . . I'm sorry!" I sputtered, then dropped the knife and ran for home, horrified by the realization of what I'd just done.

I burst into our empty house, locked myself in the bathroom, and sank to the floor, miserable and frightened. I could no longer deny that I had a severe anger problem, and that I'd never achieve my dream of being a doctor with an uncontrollable temper. I admitted to myself there was no way I could control it by myself. "Lord, please, you've got to help me," I prayed. "Take this temper away! You promised that if I ask anything in faith, you'll do it. I believe you can change me."

I slipped out and got a Bible. Back on the bathroom floor, I opened to the Book of Proverbs. The words of Proverbs 16:32— ["He who is slow to anger is better than the mighty, and he who rules his spirit than he who takes a city" (NKJV)]—convicted me, but also gave me hope. I felt God telling me that although he knew everything about me, he still loved me. . . . That because he made me, he was the only one who could change me. . . . And that he would. Gradually I stopped crying, my hands quit shaking, and I was filled with the assurance that God had answered my prayer.[2]

Dr. Carson asked God to help him say No to his temper and Yes to his calling. The arrangement between you and God and your self-control is cooperative, and the outcome is not always as immediate or dramatic as Dr. Carson's. But again, since we are going home, we might as well "get a grip" on learning to choose the right thing to do over the most pressing emotion.

Peter, of all people, could have omitted this virtue and substituted a much easier quality to work on. But Peter is not interested in covering up weaknesses or stepping around the truth. In 1 Peter 1:13, he writes, "Think clearly and exercise self-control. Look forward to the gracious salvation that will come to you when Jesus Christ is revealed to the world" (NLT). Peter is like that old farmer who knows that no matter how hard the work is, it doesn't get any easier trying to think of another way to get the job done. In all the time it takes to imagine an easy way around hard work, you might have wasted half a day and still face a whole day's worth of work left to do. Adding this quality to your to character comes as a result of at least three activities that you do in cooperation with God. If you choose to tackle the challenge of getting a grip on yourself by yourself, then you will be—how do you say it in vivid theological terms—toast. Cooperation with the Spirit of Christ is the only way to self-mastery.

Many biblical passages portray the nature and work of the devil (Matthew 6:13; 13:19, 38; John 8:44; 1 John 2:13; 1 Peter 5:8; Revelation 12:1–14). But the devil has an ally in his corner—the sinful nature *in you* that resonates with his way of life (Romans 7:14–23). As we mentioned earlier, all the beautiful attributes of God's character are woven into us (unconditional love, selflessness, generosity, etc.), along with qualities that have corrupted the human will since the Fall. One of the first and best illustrations of the need for self-control comes to us from Adam and Eve's kids—Abel and Cain. You may know the story, but notice some of the details that many overlook. "The LORD said to Cain, 'Why are you angry? Why is your face downcast? If you do what is right, will you not be accepted? But if you do not do what is right, sin is crouching at your door; it desires to have you, but you must master it'" (Genesis 4:6, 7).

God's earnest plea is for Cain to stop in his tracks. From both the inside and the outside, Satan had Cain cornered. The message of James 4:7 is clear: "Resist the devil, and he will flee from you," but also recognize the danger that lurks within. Sometimes it helps to say out loud, "No, I will not give in," or "No, if this is the voice of Satan, and by God's grace, I refuse." Practice saying No to the promptings of the evil, and by God's Spirit, you will grow more sensitive to the reality of evil. Why resist out loud?

When we say No, we really say Yes to something else. If you say No to going shopping or golfing, you are saying Yes to a visit with your family or a neighbor. If I say No to a speaking engagement, it is saying Yes to a weekend at home with my wife and kids. So, at a very basic level, saying No is choosing well in a moment of emotional, social, or spiritual confusion. It always helps to consider what you really want to say Yes to in the heat of the moment when you feel your self-control slipping.

I have tried it with doughnuts, criticism, and eating late at night. I found that I had very little self-control when it came to doughnuts. There is very little that is more destructive to health than a doughnut, and yet it is my favorite food group. As I passed by the shop at least once a day, I audibly spoke the word *No*. Something happened. My ears heard my words, and somehow I felt more resolute. I even shouted it once, but the car window was down, and I startled a person entering the shop. The customer probably thought I was yelling at her. I tell you the truth: I have experienced a lot of self-control by saying out loud what I want and don't want, what I'm willing to say Yes to and No to.

If there are two practices or exercises that might best help you add self-control to your life, it would be repentance and fasting. If you are tempted to move on to the next chapter, practice a little self-control and read beyond the stereotypes and preconceived notions you have about both. You may be surprised.

Practice repentance

What does repentance have to do with self-control? The discipline of repentance is a way to anchor your self-control by staying aware of what you are capable of and reminding yourself that you are lost without God's help. Examine the lives of people who lived the habit of repentance in Scripture, history, or your personal experience. One of my favorite examples is King Nebuchadnezzar. In Daniel 4, he tells his personal testimony about a dream that became a living nightmare. The great king went from being the mightiest ruler to a barnyard beast put out to pasture for seven years of shame. He learned the lesson of who he was and who God is. Notice the difference in his tone: "Now I, Nebuchadnezzar, praise and exalt and glorify the King of heaven, because everything he does is right and all his ways are just. And those who walk in pride he is able to humble" (Daniel 4:37).

Nebuchadnezzar did repentance the hard way. From that point on, I have no doubt that a continual battle of awareness stormed in the king about who was in control. Repent. Change your mind. Consider what books, songs, and artifacts remind you of the war that rages over your will. In my sons' room hangs a picture of a father praying over his sleeping child in the late hours of the night. Just looking at the picture never fails to bring my mind to repentance and prayer. In repentance, I discover more fully who I am and who God is.

Every time Jesus was overtly tempted, the devil targeted Christ's identity. In the wilderness, the evil one said, "If you are the Son of God . . ." Even while Jesus was on the cross, the evil one sneered through the speech of the mob, "If you are the Son of God, come down and save yourself." Know this: When Satan seeks to attack you, he aims for your identity. Paul states, "You, brothers, are not in darkness so that this day should surprise you like a thief. You are all sons of the light and sons of the day. We do not belong to the night or to the darkness. So then, let us not be like others, who are asleep, but let us be alert and self-controlled" (1 Thessalonians 5:4–6).

Practice fasting

Nothing whets your zeal for spiritual things more than a sturdy invitation to abstain from distractions. The purpose of fasting is not to deprive yourself of joy but to revive your will to choose the best way over your urges. Aside from doughnuts, I eat when I can. Food does not possess the control over me in the way that sports can. I simply get caught up in playing, watching, and planning athletic activities. I would easily choose a soccer game over mowing the lawn, preparing a sermon, or even visiting a lonely neighbor. It's wrong. Broken. Selfish. And if I fast, I choose to suspend my urgent desire to play, and instead, do something else. The result of deliberately stepping away from sports strengthens my will to say Yes to other things that are good, right, and true.

"Fasting," as Arthur Wallis says in his book *God's Chosen Fast,* "is a way of teaching our bodies to be our servants rather than our masters! What fasting may do, that nothing else can, is get us used to depending on God again—completely—for everything."[3] Dallas Willard claims that "fasting must forever center on God. It must be God-initiated and God-ordained. . . . Fasting confirms our utter dependence upon God by finding in him a source of sustenance beyond food."[4] The apostle Paul explains further: "Athletes exercise self-control in all things. . . . So I do not run aimlessly . . . but I punish my body and enslave it, so that after proclaiming to others I myself should not be disqualified" (1 Corinthians 9:25–27, NRSV).

And finally, Jesus instructed His disciples: "Whenever you fast, do not look dismal, like the hypocrites, for they disfigure their faces so as to show others that they are fasting. Truly I tell you, they have received their reward. But when you fast, put oil on your head and wash your face, so that your fasting may be seen not by others but by your Father who is in secret; and your Father who sees in secret will reward you" (Matthew 6:16–18, NRSV).

Gaining a grip on your will results from the consistent exercise of your will. Much like a muscle, your will grows, aches, and strains under the stress of work, but also grows and becomes stronger. Perhaps strong-willed people may experience recovery from addictions in a much different way from those who tend to be more compliant. For strong-willed people, the goal is to get them to admit they have a problem. For others, the problem is unmistakable—they simply need the will to work toward recovery. Once strong-willed people set their minds on a goal, they can be hard to stop.

Peter challenged the church to redirect their energies and minds on something to do, rather than focusing solely on something to resist. "Therefore, prepare your minds for action; be self-controlled; set your hope fully on the grace to be given you when Jesus Christ is revealed. As obedient children, do not conform to the evil desires you had when you lived in ignorance" (1 Peter 1:13, 14).

Think because your actions follow your mind. Give yourself to good things to do. The pressure to conform and cave in to sin and self-serving behavior is a common, continual pressure for all ages.

Psychologist Brenda Ruth performed an interesting experiment with teenagers. To show how people handle the pressure of a crowd, she gathered young people in teams of ten to undergo a test. The individuals in each group were told to raise their hand when the instructor pointed to the longest line on three separate charts. But nine of the teenagers had been previously told to vote for the second longest line. Only one person in each group had not been prompted to choose the second line. The lines were obviously not even close to the same length. The students forewarned how to vote went first, choosing the second longest line. Seventy-five percent of the time the lone student could not resist voting with the crowd even though he or she knew that the first line was significantly longer.[5]

The will that moves and makes choices throughout the day is governed by a cooperation with Christ or by the random guesses of those around you. Peter challenges every pilgrim on the walk home to get a grip and exercise their will daily.

1. Associated Press, "Man Hits Woman on Way to Anger Control Class," MSNBC.com, March 1, 2008, http://www.msnbc.msn.com/d/23421960/?gt1=43001 (accessed November 5, 2009).

2. Ben Carson, *Take the Risk: Learning to Identify, Choose, and Live With Acceptable Risk* (Grand Rapids, Mich.: Zondervan, 2008), 79, 80.

3. Arthur Wallis, *God's Chosen Fast* (Fort Washington, Penn.: Christian Literature Crusade, 1986).

4. Dallas Willard, *The Spirit of the Disciplines: Understand How God Changes Lives* (New York: HarperOne, 1990), 166.

5. Jim Rudd, "The Christian Right's Lemming Run," Covenantnews.com, September 12, 2006, http://www.covenantnews.com/blog/archives/024138.html (accessed November 17, 2009).

Questions for Reflection

1. What might change in our world today if people were to add more self-control to their lives? What areas of life would be most affected positively?

2. In what area of your life do you need to practice more self-control?

3. This chapter contained a story illustrating Dr. Ben Carson's lack of self-control. How did the young Ben Carson overcome his tendency to be hot-tempered?

4. How does Cain's story capture the momentum of sin and its work in our lives? How do we seize the moments when we are clearly out of line and headed for destruction? Do you know someone who has stopped their downward fall? How did they do it? What do you think they learned?

5. Do you agree or disagree with the statement "repentance is something you feel more than something you practice"? How might a lifestyle of repentance strengthen your grip on your will? If you were to exercise your will by fasting, what would you fast from? Why?

6. Why is self-control a quality Peter considers important for those of us making our way home?

CHAPTER 8

Just Add Perseverance

"For this very reason, make every effort to add to your faith goodness; and to goodness, knowledge; and to knowledge, self-control; and to self-control, perseverance" (2 Peter 1:5, 6).

Young William Wilberforce was discouraged one night in the early 1790s after another defeat in his ten-year battle against the slave trade in England. Tired and frustrated, he opened his Bible and began to leaf through it. A piece of paper fell out and fluttered to the floor. It was a letter written by John Wesley shortly before his death. Wilberforce read it again:

> Unless the divine power has raised you up . . . I see not how you can go through your glorious enterprise in opposing that (abominable practice of slavery), which is the scandal of religion, of England, and of human nature. Unless God has raised you up for this very thing, you will be worn out by the opposition of men and devils. But if God be for you, who can be against you? Are all of them together stronger than God? Oh, be not weary of well-doing. Go on in the name of God, and in the power of His might.[1]

In his letter to Wilberforce, John Wesley captured two of the most salient skills that enable a believer to persevere (1) attention to the goal, and (2) a deep trust in God's wisdom and abilities. Without a doubt, the obstacles will sneak in and distract you from the objective. Trials will sap your sense that God is willing and able to get you through. So, everyone who endeavors to live their life of faith as though they were on a walk home must learn to persevere.

Henry Ward Beecher once said, "The difference between perseverance and obstinacy is that one comes from a strong will, and the other from a strong won't." For this reason, Peter challenges homeward-bound pilgrims to practice the exercises that build eternal virtues. Peter urges, to self-control, add perseverance. The word Peter uses for perseverance is *hupomone*. The King James Version translates this word as "patience," but that rendering does not capture the progressive nature of the word. Patience has a passive quality, much like simply enduring or accepting your circumstances. But perseverance has a progressive motion that looks forward. Perseverance accepts not just the current circumstances but even worst obstacles that bar the way ahead. Perseverance embraces the roadblocks as another step on the rocky way.

When the journey home gets dangerous and obstacles surface at every turn, what do you do? Do you turn back, hold serve, keep what you got, and don't give any more ground? Some live by the principle, "If you leap you lose." Following that principle, the only available option is to take what is available and expect no more. My guess is that's not how most people want to live, but for some, the notion of persevering is too frightening.

The choice to either quit or continue on the walk home reminds me of a young man Parker J. Palmer touted as "the Student from Hell." Dr. Palmer attended a faculty workshop on a midwestern university campus, where he was asked on the spur of the moment to be a guest lecturer. He agreed and began teaching when he encountered what he described as "the Student from Hell," a totally disengaged student, seemingly disconnected to the class. His lecture did not go well because he poured all his effort on the mysterious young man sitting in the back of the room and failed to teach the students who were paying attention. Palmer felt like a failure and just wanted to get off the campus and put the whole experience behind him. He describes what happened next:

I was desperate to get out of town, but I had to suffer through one more event, dinner with a few faculty at the president's house. There, the workshop received fresh praise, but now the praise was painful, driving me deeper into feelings of fraudulence. When the president announced the arrival of the college van that would haul me to the airport, I was flooded with relief.

I went out to the driveway, tossed my bags in the back seat of the van, climbed into the front seat, and turned to greet the driver.

It was the Student from Hell.

I am a religious person, so I commenced to pray: "I have sinned, I do sin, and given an attractive opportunity, I will probably sin again. But nothing I have ever done or plan to do merits this punishment—an hour and a half in a van with the Student from Hell."

We backed out of the driveway and wound our way through the neighborhood, staring ahead in silence. When we reached the freeway, the driver suddenly spoke, "Dr. Palmer, is it OK if we talk?"

Every atom in my body screamed "No!" But my mouth, which was trained in the suburbs, said, "Sure, fine, yes, you bet."

I will always remember the conversation that followed. The student's father was an unemployed laborer and an alcoholic who thought that his son's desire to finish college and become some sort of professional was utter nonsense.

The young man lived with his father, who berated him daily for his foolishness: "The world is out to get people like us, and college is part of the scam. Drop out, get a fast-food job, save whatever you can, and settle for it. That's how it's always been, and that's how it'll always be."[2]

Everyone who has a heart beating in his or her chest just wants to shout, "NO! Don't believe it! Press on! You can do this! Break the cycle of living by dwarfed goals!" "Your courage to finish college is just behind your willingness to ignore negative thoughts about the future."

The Bible is filled with encouragement to persevere and examples of people who do, but very little information about the nuances about the process of those who press on. Why so little information about how to persevere? Perhaps perseverance is one aspect of the journey that you should not try to tease apart or overexplain—but just do. Just press through this trial and you will see. Just hang on to your hope and get through the fog. You can assess the experience on the other side. People who must understand every nuance of life rarely have the courage to live. Those who endeavor to persevere, discover enough on the downhill side of trials to smile. They learn that God's power combined with their stubborn resolve to stay with Him is more than enough to make the journey worthwhile.

In Luke 8:15, Jesus described the work of the seed to grow and bear fruit as perseverance: "The seed in the good soil, these are the ones who have heard the word in an honest and good heart, and hold it fast, and bear fruit with perseverance" (NASB). I love to watch children who grow seeds at school in their little Styrofoam cups with holes poked in the bottom. As soon as one kid notices the supple green stem popping through the surface, all the classmates are tempted to help their plant along. They pry a little dirt to the side, thinking they help their emerging plant, but in fact they are killing the tiny sprout. What enables the sprout to break through the ground is the strength it gains through perseverance. Without the muscle to break the ground, the plant will die. Making it easier for the plant to break the surface only makes it impossible for the plant to survive. The same is true for us. The journey home gives us opportunities to grow in grace and become sturdy in our faith in God's plan for our eternal life. We grow to love and value this walk home by negotiating through the challenges that bar our way to the destination. It's not a game, but it is the reality of living in a world of sin.

Paul describes the process of this kind of growth in Romans 5:3–5, "Not only this, but we also exult in our tribulations, knowing that tribulation brings about perseverance; and perseverance, proven character; and proven character, hope; and hope does not disappoint, because the love of God has been poured out within our hearts through the Holy Spirit who was given to us" (NASB).

Perseverance is the key element embedded in the growth process, and Paul claims that God does this out of love! But God is not some sick exercise trainer screaming at you, "No pain, no gain!" Perhaps one of the most encouraging passages from Peter's pen is this:

> In this you greatly rejoice, though now for a little while you may have had to suffer grief in all kinds of trials. These have come so that your faith—of greater worth than gold, which perishes even though refined by fire—may be proved genuine and may result in praise, glory and honor when Jesus Christ is revealed. Though you have not seen him, you love him; and even though you do not see him now, you believe in him and are filled with an inexpressible and glorious joy, for you are receiving the goal of your faith, the salvation of your souls (1 Peter 1:6–9).

Throughout the Scriptures, biblical giants cheer us on to persevere. John the revelator includes the words of an angel explaining how believers finally overcome the obstacles of the evil one: "They overcame him by the blood of the Lamb and by the word of their testimony; they did not love their lives so much as to shrink from death" (Revelation 12:11).

John saw the end and described the victorious band of redeemed who made the walk home: "Here is the perseverance of the saints who keep the commandments of God and their faith in Jesus" (Revelation 14:12, NASB).

For years, I, and many others, have heralded the two characteristics of the remnant: keep the commandments and have the testimony of Jesus. But in our earnest desire to proclaim the truth, we pass over the quality that gets us there—perseverance. We will never obey God or possess an enduring faith in Christ without learning the hard way of perseverance. Chances are high that today you face a challenge, an obstacle to your journey home, that continually distracts you or seems to block your way with fear and uncertainty. Remember, perseverance is a by-product of practice. And sometimes it is solely a matter of wearing out the opponent with the knowledge that no matter what happens, you are going home.

The story is told that Andrew Jackson's childhood friends could not fathom how he became a successful general and then the president of the United States. They could list dozens of men that possessed greater talent who never succeeded. One friend is rumored to have said, " 'Why, Jim Brown, who lived right down the road from Jackson, was not only smarter but he could throw Andy three times out of four in a wrestling match. But look where Andy is now.' Another friend responded, 'Why was there a fourth time? Don't the rules say, three times and you are out?' The other responded saying, 'Sure, they were supposed to, but not Andy. He would never admit that he was done—he might of gotten "throwed" but he would never stay "throwed." ' "[3] Apparently, the first matches would tire out his opponent, and Andrew Jackson would win the final attempt by persevering.

Let us wear out the enemy of souls by staying on the road home, no matter what comes our way. The final fight is already won. Consider a few practices or exercises that enable you to add to your self-control, perseverance.

Practice fellowship

The community of faith is made up of fellow travelers who endure, but none do so alone. Reflect on the times in your journey when you faced seemingly insurmountable trials, and I would daresay you did not make it through in isolation. Invite people who know Christ to encourage you and help you press through. I know prayer groups and accountability partners who urge each other through the hard parts of the walk home. Alone, we think and overanalyze our predicaments. We quietly rationalize another way to go, and before we know it, we have stopped walking. When I go running by myself, I never run faithfully or as far as I will run with a friend. There is no need to get scientific about it—don't walk home alone!

Practice enduring prayer

As a youth pastor, I learned how praying for young people in an enduring way deepened my capacity to persevere. Paul taught me, "Pray in the Spirit on all occasions with all kinds of prayers and requests. With this in mind, be alert and always keep on praying for all the saints" (Ephesians 6:18–20). Two aspects of this passage encourage me. First, I struggled initially to call the young people in my church "saints." "Rascals" seemed more appropriate. But pray for those little rascals and you begin to see what Paul sees—saints. "In all my prayers for all of you, I always pray with joy because of your partnership in the gospel from the first day until now, being confident of this, that he who began a good work in you will carry it on to completion until the day of Christ Jesus" (Philippians 1:4–6).

Second, I learned that praying regularly for young people taught me never to give up on them—to try to see the sleeping hero inside of them. And God urges us to practice this because sometimes the realization that others are not giving up on them may cause people to not give up on themselves. Keep praying! In fact, Ellen White encourages us to pray this way:

"Were not miracles wrought by Christ and His apostles? The same compassionate Saviour lives today. And He is willing to listen to the prayer of faith as when He walked visibly among men. The natural cooperates with the supernatural. It is part of God's plan to grant us, in answer to the prayer of faith, that which He would not bestow did we not thus ask."[4]

If you look at my desk, you'll see that on it I have written in permanent ink the names of every young person's name in my church. Each day I lift them up by name, praying for them to endure and know the risen Christ. I pray for the experiences in life that will stretch them and cause them to struggle with their faith that it might be strong. As they find their strength in Christ, my ultimate prayer for them is that they will live their lives on earth as though they are walking home.

The story of Florence Chadwick reminds us how to persevere on the way home. She was the first woman to swim the English Channel in both directions. In 1952, she tried to swim from Catalina Island to the coast of California. The most significant challenge was not the distance as much as it was the cold temperatures of the Pacific Ocean. Adding to the bone-chilling cold water was the fog that hung over the region, making it impossible to see land. She swam like a champion for fifteen hours but gave up within a half mile of her destination because she could not see land through the fog. Afterward she told a reporter, "I'm not trying to make excuses, but if I could have seen land, I might have made it." With that notion fixed firmly in her mind, she made another attempt, but again the fog came in and obscured her ability to see the end goal. But this time she kept swimming, reminding herself that land was there and she was within reach. Confident in what she could not see, but knew in her heart, she bravely swam to victory, breaking the men's record by two hours.

It helps to know there is land ahead, just beyond the pain, the struggle, or the tragedy that is before us. There in the fog of our journey, we reject the lie that we are lost and going nowhere and believe the truth that we are almost home.

I'll leave you with this familiar hymn ringing in your heart:

There's a land that is fairer than day,
And by faith we can see it afar;
For the Father waits over the way,
To prepare us a dwelling place there.

In the sweet by and by,
We shall meet on that beautiful shore;
In the sweet by and by,
We shall meet on that beautiful shore.[5]

---

1. Letter from John Wesley to Wilberforce.
2. Parker J. Palmer, *The Courage to Teach: Exploring the Inner Landscape of a Teacher's Life* (Hoboken, N.J.: Jossey-Bass, 1997), 44, 45.
3. Andrew Jackson anecdote.
4. Ellen G. White, *The Great Controversy* (Nampa, Idaho: Pacific Press® Publishing Association, 1950), 525.
5. Lyrics to "Sweet By and By" by Sanford F. Bennett.

Questions for Reflection

1. Think of people who are persevering. Is it because of their persisting "will" or their stubborn "won't"? How does their proactive determination for the "will" affect their lives?

2. The story "The Student From Hell" contains a call to refuse to succumb to fear but to press forward in hope. Do you know people struggling with voices that urge them to give up? What words of encouragement might inspire them to persevere?

3. Do you agree or disagree with the statement that "perseverance is something that is done rather than something one prepares for or thinks about." Why? What kind of thinking is involved in the lives of people such as Job, Joseph, and Sarah?

4. This chapter relates the quality of perseverance to those who are victorious at the end of time. How would a person with perseverance be a light or a witness to others at the end of time? What are some ways you imagine this being a reality?

5. In Romans 5:3–5, Paul comments on the work that perseverance does to grow us toward a rich, enduring hope that is eternal. When in your life have you experienced the fruit of perseverance?

6. As you make your way home, what specific area of your life is demanding the practice of perseverance? How might you remind yourself to stay the course?

7. For some, the spiritual discipline of fellowship is a welcome opportunity, through collaboration, to share each other's burdens. How might a group's support help you, or someone else, practice endurance in a challenge you are struggling with?

8. As you reflect on the story of Florence Chadwick, imagine the lights and the shoreline just ahead as your goal. Pray for your immediate circumstances with the idea that you are almost home and see what happens.

CHAPTER 9

Just Add Godliness

"For this very reason, make every effort to add to your faith goodness; and to goodness, knowledge; and to knowledge, self-control; and to self-control, perseverance; and to perseverance, godliness" (2 Peter 1:5, 6).

When I coached baseball, we practiced on a full-size high school field where the fence that marked a home run seemed like a mile for the little boys and girls that I was working with. I would tell them that their fence was much closer, but they couldn't seem to get beyond how impossibly far away the end of the outfield was. Their hitting became worse, and with every ball that barely trickled to the outfield, their courage waned and so did their power.

The next time we practiced hitting, I brought out a makeshift plastic fence and placed it right where the fence would be in their upcoming games—and it transformed their hitting. They now were trying because they saw that it was possible. And the same is true for us in the way we perceive our walk home with God. Perhaps godliness is a home-run fence line so far out of reach we can't even imagine such a virtue applied to us. If being godly is equated with being God, then nobody in his right mind even tries. But after we understand the word better, the impossible fence is brought closer.

Peter's charge to add to their perseverance, godliness, causes many to freeze up or simply disengage. For *godliness,* Peter used *eusebia,* which is a hard word to translate, but is the kind of person who is able to look simultaneously in two different directions: upward to God as well as sideways to people. Another way to describe godliness is *to worship well.* Clearly, the word implies a balanced tension between two worlds—the heavenly world and the world we live in.

Raphael painted *The School of Athens* portraying similar tensions between two views of the universe. Plato stands with his finger pointing up to the heavens and next to him is Aristotle, his young sparring partner in philosophy, pointing to the earth. And gathered around the large room are the great philosophers of Hellenistic thinking. We would need many chapters to unpack fully the ideas of both Plato and Aristotle; however, my guess is that the few people who would enjoy doing that are probably not reading this book. So suffice it to say that one view is a mystical view of the universe while the other is a realistic reference point.

It may be that a godly person is someone who lives simultaneously in both worlds. Clearly, Jesus embodied the perfect expression of godliness in His incarnation, but remember that it is Peter who charges us to add this seemingly impossible virtue. This apostle, most noted for his wild swings between greatness and evil, believes the virtue of godliness is characteristic of those going home. And the question to ask next is not, How do I become godly, but who do I know who walks this way? Enoch comes to mind—a man who modeled the idea of walking home with God.

Enoch

At last, if there is anyone who may tell the story of the walk home it is Enoch, yet only a handful of other people in Scripture are described as having walked with God. Furthermore, who can relate to Enoch? Of all the people to be like, who would dare be of the mind-set to choose Enoch as their mentor? David. Joseph. Paul. Hey, dare to be a Daniel—

but Enoch? When did being ready for translation become such an unreachable dream?

I never thought much about Enoch because if there were anyone in Scripture I felt I could not relate to, it was the guy who walked with God and vanished.

During a high school class discussion on Abraham Lincoln, the teacher asked about his various accomplishments and then asked, "Do you know when he died?"

Benji, the quiet young man who was sitting at the back, replied, "April 15, 1865."

Everyone turned to look at Benji. The teacher affirmed, "That's right, and—" but before he could move the class forward, another student interrupted, "How did you know that?"

Benji offered a cryptic answer, "I just do." The teacher again tried to put the derailed train back on track when another student launched, "What about George Washington?"

Almost without taking a breath, he responded, "December 14, 1799—he died of pneumonia."

"You know how he died?" Kyle asked. "Does anyone else think that's odd?"

The class tossed out names of presidents at Benji, and he knocked them out of the park:

"John Adams, July 4, 1826."

"Thomas Jefferson, July 4, 1826."

"No way—two presidents on the same day—on July 4; he's making it up. Get an encyclopedia." They checked; Benji was right.

John Quincy Adams, February 23, 1848.

Martin Van Buren, July 24, 1862.

At that point, the game played out of control, but the teacher let Benji's classmates have a go at him.

William McKinley, September 14, 1901.

Ulysses S. Grant, July 23, 1885.

Reggie erupted, "Aha! Grant was a general. Gotcha!"

In the middle of his victory dance, he noticed everyone staring at him in disbelief. Janet, the one with the encyclopedia, said, "Sit down, Reggie. He was a general *and* a president and the date is correct!"

Zachary Taylor, July 9, 1850.

Dwight Eisenhower, March 28, 1969.

Roosevelt—to which Benji replied, "Ted or Frank?"

Everyone in the class had two questions they were dying to ask, "How could someone memorize all those dates?" Answer: Perhaps Benji was a genius with numbers. The other question haunted them even more than how someone would do it, but why someone would even try. They asked both questions.

"I help my dad mow the lawns at the cemetery. I just started reading the dates, looking at how long the people had lived, and then I'd try to imagine what the world was like at the time of their death. It passed the time."

Later, one of Benji's assignments for Bible class was to do a character sketch on a person in the Bible that you identified with. Benji chose Enoch and entitled his report, "No Tombstone for Enoch." Benji claimed, "Enoch is a guy who walked with God and never stopped." I daresay that if you asked a thousand Christians today who they identified with the most in the Bible, very few would choose Enoch.

Peter—definitely. Perhaps Mary—it would depend on which Mary. I know Christians who adopt a sliver of Hindu theology when life hits them hard, and they believe they are a reincarnated version of Job. Sarah—sure. But Enoch? Enoch's out there—literally (somewhere). We admire Enoch, but we don't identify with him. We certainly don't hold him up as an example or standard because he is much too holy to walk behind. Perhaps the less we know of Enoch, the more mysterious and mystical he becomes. All we really know about Enoch is that he "walked with God," and because he was so holy, God took him to heaven. But I wonder about how Enoch's walk at the end of time (before the Flood) might mirror the journey of believers today.

Every walk begins with a few first steps. One question I have about Enoch's walk with God is, How did his journey begin? Where did Enoch start? Unfortunately, the Bible doesn't offer many details about Enoch, but it does say something about his first steps. First of all, we know that Enoch was born the son of Jared. In Genesis 5:18–20, "When Jared had lived 162 years, he became the father of Enoch. And after he became the father of Enoch, Jared lived 800 years and had other sons and daughters. Altogether, Jared lived 962 years, and then he died."

So, Enoch, like everyone else, except Adam and Eve, was born. Big deal. But then Enoch had a defining moment. Do you know what I mean by a "defining moment"? A pivotal experience that changed his way of thinking and his way of walking. What are some of your defining moments? It is helpful to ruminate on them every once in a while.

One event. One decision. One true or false move can make you or break you. Now, people who had experienced pivotal events in their lives have been known to recover or even return to old patterns. So just because someone has an epiphany doesn't mean he can't become apathetic. And just because someone makes a really bad decision and his life becomes broken, it doesn't mean he misses out on ever being restored. But it is true that typically some event, experience, or revelation initiates a new way of thinking as well as a new way to live.

Defining moments don't have to be dramatic. Change can emerge from normal, simple experiences that simply pivot your life in a different direction.

Consider Enoch's defining moment, "When Enoch had lived 65 years, he became the father of Methuselah. And after he became the father of Methuselah, Enoch walked with God 300 years and had other sons and daughters. Altogether, Enoch lived 365 years. Enoch walked with God; then he was no more, because God took him away" (Genesis 5:21–24).

Did you see it? Mr. Perfect (Enoch) had a kid, and like everyone else out there, it brought him to his knees. Enoch's life isn't a shiny path of flawless behavior but a hand-to-hand walk with God, brought on by parenthood. Enoch had a child and the experience transformed him. (I'm not suggesting that the way to a deep abiding relationship with God is to go and have a baby—please hear me on this!) But at the age of sixty-five, when Enoch became a parent, something clicked, and he became devoted to a deeper walk with God than before. Notice Ellen White's commentary on this event:

> After the birth of his first son, Enoch reached a higher experience; he was drawn into a closer relationship with God. He realized more fully his own obligations and responsibility as a son of God. And as he saw the child's love for its father, its simple trust in his protection; as he felt the deep, yearning tenderness of his own heart for that first-born son, he learned a precious lesson of the wonderful love of God to men in the gift of His Son, and the confidence which the children of God may repose in their heavenly Father.[1]

Enoch's walk pivoted when he had a boy named Methuselah. He watched the way his son looked at him and adored him, identified with him, and was loyally devoted to him. Sometimes parents think we understand God's grace because we experience this unconditional love for our children; that is true—but for Enoch, he was drawn closer to God because of the way he saw his son love him. He learned about intimacy with God by looking at the way his child looked at him. And he longed to adore God with the same kind of devotion.

Remember what John said to the church: "How great is the love the Father has lavished on us, that we should be called children of God! And that is what we are!" (1 John 3:1).

The second question I would ask about Enoch's walk with God is, What did Enoch's walk look like?

Everyone has a style to the way they walk. Sometimes you may be too far away to recognize a person's face, but you know who it is by the style of his walk. Enoch had a walk. In Scripture, I could only find two qualities about the way Enoch walked—that's it. The first quality of Enoch's walk is his talk. In Jude 14, 15, we read, "Enoch, the seventh from Adam, prophesied about these men: 'See, the Lord is coming with thousands upon thousands of his holy ones to judge everyone, and to convict all the ungodly of all the ungodly acts they have done in the ungodly way, and of all the harsh words ungodly sinners have spoken against him.' "

All we really have on Enoch is what he would talk about. He saw the world steeped in sin. It was revealed to him that his son Methuselah was going to see the world get so bad that God would have to send a flood and start over. Clearly, Enoch had much to say about God, sin, and the coming of the Lord in judgment. Enoch would not have been everybody's buddy. A friend—yes. The father of Methuselah and the son of Jared joined hands with God and started walking home because he came to believe in a new Eden, and he knew the world was coming to an end.

As I said at the beginning of this book, sin is wrong. It breaks. It kills. It lies. It robs us of our true purpose. Downplaying the horror of sin waters down the power of Christ at Calvary. What do you think made Calvary necessary? There is no need to fixate on it. But the more we water down the evilness of sin, the more we make the grace of God irrelevant. Enoch's walk is characterized by strong words about sin and a passionate message about going home. Enoch called it straight, not moralizing from his own mountaintop experience but pleading for people to embrace the grace of God and the forgiveness he knew so well.

The second quality that Scripture reveals about Enoch's walk is his heart. The only other thing mentioned in the Bible about Enoch is that he sought to please God: "By faith Enoch was taken from this life, so that he did not experience death; he could not be found, because God had taken him away. For before he was taken, he was commended as one who pleased God. And without faith it is impossible to please God, because anyone who comes to him must believe that he exists and that he rewards those who earnestly seek him" (Hebrews 11:5, 6).

Go back to what kids teach us about the kingdom. Look at the glee in their faces as we celebrate the first time they write their names. Or how they light up when we cheer for them as they sing in the Christmas program. Children are perfectionists when it comes to pleasing others. They simple love it. When we remember how children love to please their parents, Enoch doesn't have to be so ultrasaintly in our minds. What makes Enoch's walk with God so rich and enduring (really enduring) is the simplicity. Enoch saw how to love God the way a child loves a parent. He looked around and saw how sin had broken this world, and he longed for home. He spoke up and lived a life of walking with God as though his Father were walking him home through the dark part of town. He called for others to join the journey. His life calls out today, "Come home. Come meet my Father. Grab His hand; it is big enough for all of us. Let's leave the darkness and walk home."

Is it safe to ask whether a walk like Enoch's could start today? Could you begin by resting in the truth that you are a child of the King? As you walk home, you will hate sin and will make plain to others the matchless grace of God. Tell your simple story. That's probably what Enoch did. And, what if each day you were to ask yourself, What would make my Father in heaven smile today? What if pleasing the Father prompted every move of your mission, your work, and your study and play? How might the style of your walk be different from what it is now?

Enoch is not entirely alone. In fact, many have walked hand in hand with God and with people—but one common theme seems to emerge from their storied lives, and it is the idea that they embraced weirdness. "Noah found favor in the eyes of the LORD. This is the account of Noah. Noah was a righteous man, blameless among the people of his time, and he walked with God" (Genesis 6:8, 9).

In Noah's day, the world had become corrupt, but it had not decayed the way we see it today. The earth still looked much like it did when God created it. People were big, bright, and beautiful. People had come to trust in their own beauty and knowledge, so much so that they thought they had no need of their Creator. They scoffed and chided Noah's simple faith. The antediluvians expressed a self-absorbed elitism that smirked and made snide comments about faith in God.

Noah was willing to be in the minority. Is it possible that we have heard this story so much that we are so familiar with it that we miss how outrageous it is? But step back and look at the whole of Scripture, and we will see that it is filled with moments where godliness runs counter to the customary.

Ask Gideon about the unexpected instructions from God: "Hey Gideon, choose your army based not upon the strength of your soldiers or their skill in warfare but, instead, choose your army by the way they drink water. Oh yeah, and when you go to fight the enemy, take a flashlight and a Tupperware pitcher as weapons. Trust Me, it works every time."

Or ask Joshua: "Hey Joshua, march the saints around the city seven times and blow the trumpets and just yell really loud and the walls will fall—trust me."

Ask David: how much more of an underdog could David have been against Goliath, and yet someone was whispering in the young man's ear that the giant was going down.

When you are trapped between a raging army out for blood and a giant sea, it's just not expected to reason, "Hmm—God wants me to divide the sea with my staff so we can walk across the seabed to the other side." Over and over again, this beautiful, wonderful God makes it clear that He has a way of doing things—and is unexpected.

Those who add to their perseverance, godliness and learn to walk with God are often forced to suspend, if not strip away, their presuppositions about the way things need to be and how they should happen.

Perhaps the most abnormal feature of Noah's walk is captured in this one short sentence: "Noah did everything just as God commanded him" (Genesis 6:22). Flawless? No. But Noah obeyed and worked faithfully for God, in such a way that he has been described as one who "walked with God." Oh, and by the way, if you are still wondering whether people who walk with God never struggle or even fail, take a moment and read one and Noah's less godlike stories in Genesis 9.

Noah had his head in heaven and his hands at work on earth, pleading and working to save anyone who had the desire to go home.

Practice having a double focus by making a sacrifice or taking a leap of faith

Are there any godly people here on earth today? Are there any today who have a double focus? People who gaze both toward home and toward people?

When people walk away from self-serving careers to follow God's call—that's having a double focus. When Christian believers have to explain to personal accountants why so much of their income goes to their church—that's a double focus. When a college student is so moved by his own mission experience that he sells his car or computer to pay for someone else to go on a mission trip—that student has a double focus.

Practice godliness by worshiping well

This week when you go to the house of God to worship, take notice of who is there. First, God promises to meet you, so pay attention to Him. When I walked into the foyer of the church a while back, I noticed a college student in front of me with her hand on the door, pausing before she entered the sanctuary. I didn't have to ask, but I did, "Are you ready?" She answered, "Now, I am." Because the routine can snatch away your sense of awe, take a moment and pause to remember to whom you are singing, praying, giving, and learning to be like.

Also, you may notice someone else to pay attention to. Ideally, there will be people. Reflect on the ones you know, their life, their journey, their strengths, and even their weaknesses. With grace and mercy, pray for them because as wonderful or annoying as many of us are, we are just trying to go home. Cover them before God with a prayer for mercy and strength. But experience the beauty of a collective body of believers all together for a breather—a time out to remember who we are and where we are all going.

A walk with God is not out of reach. It may seem strange at first to have one's focus on the clouds of heaven and simultaneously on the needs of people. Godliness is this tender tension between two worlds so far apart in character, but so inseparably tied together by the mercy of God. Maybe you have heard the saying, "You can be so heavenly minded you are no earthly good." I believe nothing could be further from the truth. The people I know doing the most good on earth are the travelers who are on the way home.

---

1. White, *Patriarchs and Prophets* (Nampa, Idaho: Pacific Press® Publishing Association, 1958), 84.

Questions for Reflection

1. When you think of adding the quality of godliness to your life, what are some of your immediate reactions to the word *godly*? Of all the things you pray to achieve, is this typically one of them? Why? Why not?

2. Who do you know who might be described as "godly" people? Why do you and others describe them this way?

3. What Bible characters would you include in your list of top five godly people? (Don't count Jesus—He is a given.) Were these people close to flawless? Why do you think about them as godly?

4. Why do you think Enoch is a hard person to mirror as a mentor or person you want to be like? As you think more about his experience, does he become more normal or less?

5. How does becoming a child of God transform the very mind-set of a believer today?

6. How are Enoch's qualities needed today? In what sense is our world ready for a few more people like Enoch? How was the world in Noah's era like the world we live in today?

7. As you practice godliness, the vision for the here and the hereafter, consider what sacrifice or leap of faith you might take in the coming days.

8. Think about what it would look like to be heavenly minded in a way that was an earthly good.

CHAPTER 10

Just Add Brotherly Kindness

"For this very reason, make every effort to add to your faith goodness; and to goodness, knowledge; and to knowledge, self-control; and to self-control, perseverance; and to perseverance, godliness; and to godliness, brotherly kindness" (2 Peter 1:5–7).

I've always wanted to write about or speak about kindness using the title "Brotherly Kindness and Other Oxymorons."

Some of my favorite oxymorons:

- Exact estimate
- Fat-free dessert
- Good grief
- Sanitary landfill
- Small crowd
- Soft rock
- Peacekeeping force
- Political science
- Definite maybe
- Act naturally
- Same difference
- Twelve-ounce pound cake

- Airline food
- Virtual reality
- Timeless moment
- Brotherly kindness

Brothers are not always known for their kindness. However, because both of my brothers are even bigger and meaner than I am, I can only say relatively nice things about them—however inaccurate those words may be. Actually, during my seasons of thoughtless wandering, my older brother has demonstrated kindness to me that transcends friendship. My younger brother constantly reminds me of how great I am not, which I'm sure has some ultimate purpose. In truth, both of my brothers are generous and kind people.

The word Peter uses for "brotherly kindness" is the Greek word *philadelphia,* which is literally translated "love of the brethren." Matthew Henry describes this virtue as, "a tender affection to all our fellow-Christians, who are children of the same Father, servants of the same Master, members of the same family, travelers to the same country, and heirs of the same inheritance, and therefore are to be loved with a pure heart fervently."[1]

The Scriptures include the theme that Christians—all Christians—are part of a family. To add the adjectives "brotherly or sisterly" to kindness means we perceive and behave as though we are all related, because we are.

Peter qualifies this kind of kindness as a sincere expression, "deep" and "from the heart." "Now that you have purified yourselves by obeying the truth so that you have sincere love for your brothers, love one another deeply, from the heart" (1 Peter 1:22).

The instructions continue.

- Keep on loving each other as brothers (Hebrews 13:1).
- Be devoted to one another in brotherly love. Honor one an-

other above yourselves (Romans 12:10).

- Everyone who believes that Jesus is the Christ is born of God, and everyone who loves the father loves his child as well. This is how we know that we love the children of God: by loving God and carrying out his commands (1 John 5:1, 2).

In the community of faith, we are commanded to demonstrate grace by the way we treat each other. When I read the following passage in Galatians, the message disturbed me: "Let us not become weary in doing good, for at the proper time we will reap a harvest if we do not give up. Therefore, as we have opportunity, let us do good to all people, especially to those who belong to the family of believers" (Galatians 6:9, 10).

Don't get tired of doing good. That makes sense. The next phrase promises a harvest. You reap what you sow; this is basic Bible truth. Do good to all people. Amen! Everyone is valued in the eyes of God. "Whether they are hell-bent or heaven-sent," my old Texas pastor would roar, "love 'em all as God loves them." But when Paul writes, "especially to those who belong to the family of believers," I choke. Is he kidding? There is something wrong with placing the word *especially* in the text, distinguishing who should receive kindness the most. Disturbing. But the more I think about it, the more it makes sense. Why in the world would anyone want to be a part of the church if we are not kind to each other? Because we demonstrate to the world what loving each other looks like, people want to become "related" to us.

The greatest acts of kindness ought to be pervasive within our churches, not at the exclusion of "outsiders," but so people will see us for who we really are. No bait and switch. No more being really nice during the evangelistic meetings but acting nasty to new believers before they even have time to dry off from their baptism. Imagine a church that lived for one year devoted to practicing the message of kindness to the body of believers. What would a church like that look like?

But brotherly kindness is to be extended to *all* who come in contact with us as we walk home. The journey will cause us to cross paths with many who don't understand our Father, our journey, or our destination. But learning to seize the opportunities becomes one of our greatest virtues. Julio Diaz truly has the virtue of brotherly kindness:

Julio Diaz, a 31-year-old Bronx social worker, just wanted to do what he did every night on the way home from work: grab a quick bite to eat at his favorite diner. Only one thing stood in his way from doing just that—a mugger. When Diaz stepped off the train and onto the subway platform, a teenager ran up to him, pulled out a knife, and demanded Diaz hand over his wallet. Realizing it wasn't worth a fight, Diaz fished the wallet out of his pocket and gave it to the boy. Much to the mugger's surprise, Diaz decided to go the extra mile. As the teen ran away, Diaz called out, "If you're going to be robbing people for the rest of the night, you might as well take my coat to keep you warm."

The boy stopped in his tracks, shocked. Diaz explained that it was quite clear the teen needed money, so he told him to keep the wallet, take the coat, and if he wanted, grab a bite to eat with Diaz. The boy was too shocked to say no.

As the two ate dinner at Diaz's favorite diner, the teen marveled over how many dishwashers and waitresses offered Diaz a wave or a friendly word. He figured Diaz owned the place. When the boy shared his observation, Diaz smiled and said, "Haven't you been taught you should be nice to everybody?"

"Yeah," the teen replied, "but I didn't think people actually behaved that way."

The two continued to talk about life and other matters. When the bill finally came, Diaz told the boy that he needed his wallet to pay. The boy handed it back without thinking twice. Diaz paid for the meal and offered the teen twenty dollars. He also asked that his would-be mugger surrender the knife—which he did.[2]

Peter's challenge to add kindness is an attempt to put flesh on our greatest thoughts and feelings about grace. In fact, *kindness* is the word used to describe what God was doing for us in the incarnation of Christ (Ephesians 2:7). Christ's coming to earth and becoming one with us is, in the most tangible, practical sense, a gift of kindness. God knows how compelling His children are when they extend themselves with deeds that are kind. Even the wise guy in Proverbs claimed, "The desire of a man is his kindness" (Proverbs 19:22, KJV). Moreover, Paul urges us to clothe or cover our lives with tangible grace, and, not surprisingly, one of those qualities is kindness: "Therefore, as God's chosen people, holy and dearly loved, clothe yourselves with compassion, kindness, humility, gentleness and patience" (Colossians 3:12).

So as you make your way home, stop to give kindness away!

Practice kind words

I love the story of the young father in a supermarket who was pushing a shopping cart with his little son strapped in the seat. The little boy was fussing, irritable, and crying. The other shoppers gave the pair a wide berth because the child would pull cans off the shelf and throw them out of the cart. The father seemed to be very calm; as he continued down each aisle, he murmured gently, "Easy now, Donald. Keep calm, Donald. Steady, boy. It's all right, Donald."

A mother who was passing by was greatly impressed by this young father's solicitous attitude. She said, "You certainly know how to talk to an upset child—quietly and gently."

And then bending down to the little boy, she said, "What seems to be the trouble, Donald?"

"Oh, no," said the father. "He's Henry. I'm Donald."

Sometimes, all it takes is a few simple words of encouragement to keep everything under control. Ideally, brothers and sisters would do great good if people did not have to whisper words of encouragement to themselves to hear it. Words are powerful. A few words spoken can help stir kindness, but a few harsh words of criticism can destroy. I often reflect on what it would be like if all believers simply obeyed the counsel of Paul when he says, "Do not let any unwholesome talk come out of your mouths, but only what is helpful for building others up according to their needs, that it may benefit those who listen" (Ephesians 4:29). Can you imagine how hard that would be to do? Even more, can you even conceive of how many would be restored, built up, redeemed, or returned from despair if we simply did this one thing?

Sister Helen Mrosla had a life-changing impact on her junior high math students, and particularly on a young boy named Mark. The young boy and his classmates worked hard; and by the end of the week, everyone in the class became a little grumpy. Taking a break from the work, Sister Mrosla asked each person in the class to list the nicest thing they think about each member of the class and hand the list to her. She then compiled the lists so that each student had a list of what classmates especially liked about him or her. Years later, Mark was killed in Vietnam. After the funeral, most of his old classmates joined Sister Mrosla and went to Chuck's house for lunch. Mark's parents were also invited. While they were eating, Mark's father took a wallet out of his pocket. "They found this on Mark when he was killed," he said. He gently opened the wallet and carefully removed a folded piece of paper that had obviously been refolded and taped over the seasons. On the piece of paper was the list of kind things Mark's classmates said about him. Clearly, the words of kindness became a source of strength and hope for Mark in unimaginable seasons of trauma.

One of Mark's classmates, Charlie, smiled and said, "I keep my list in my desk drawer."

Chuck, also a friend in class didn't say anything, but his wife chimed in, adding, "Chuck put his in our wedding album."

"I put mine in my diary," Marilyn said.

Vicky, another classmate, reached into her pocketbook and unfolded her frayed list. No one needed to say more. Sticks and stones may break your bones but words conquer the darkest night. It becomes more difficult to give up when people are cheering your name. When people who believe the best about you say it, it's hard to forget how much you matter to God and people. Perhaps this week you can sit down and pen words that convey grace, encouragement, and hope to someone you know is struggling.

Practice kind deeds

Brotherly kindness is often just as powerful seen rather than heard. You know people who don't want to be on stage or possess the spotlight. These people don't need accolades or pre-eminence. Their greatest joy is to give, to work, to do things for others.

I remember being on a marketing committee whose purpose was to present a high school's positive image to the community. Brainstorming turned up a great many marketing schemes to sell the image of a school that serves. Most of the time had been spent on crafting a brochure, when a wise old grandparent suggested, "We ought to stop wasting time on producing a brochure and get our kids serving the community. We should stop talking and actually get something done. Then maybe we might have something to write a brochure about. My guess is, that if we were to be busy doing service in the community, we wouldn't need a brochure, or even a committee like this one, for that matter." Amen.

The virtue of brotherly kindness grows on us and in us as we practice service, fellowship, generous giving, and a whole host of activities as we make our journey home. It is likely that two thousand years have not changed the need for a community of kindness. Consider the timeless admonition from the book of Hebrews: "Let us hold unswervingly to the hope we profess, for he who promised is faithful. And let us consider how we may spur one another on toward love and good deeds. Let us not give up meeting together, as some are in the habit of doing, but let us encourage one another—and all the more as you see the Day approaching" (Hebrews 10:23–25).

---

1. *Matthew Henry's Commentary on the Whole Bible,* s.v. "brotherly love," CD-ROM, Biblesoft, Inc., 2006.

2. "A Victim Treats His Mugger Right," NPR.org, March 28, 2008, http://www.npr.org/templates/story/story.php?storyId=89164759 (accessed November 11, 2009).

Questions for Reflection

1. What are some of your favorite oxymorons?

2. Think of a season in your journey when someone extended brotherly or sisterly kindness to you? How did you receive it? What impact did the experience have on you?

3. When you think of the reasons why many avoid Christianity, how much of it has to do with Christ? How much of their resistance has to do with Christians? Read Galatians 6:9, 10 and notice the word especially at the end. Does this seem backward to you? Why or why not?

4. What might be the results in the church if believers were to become famous for taking care of one another with genuine kindness?

5. This week, make a list of people you are going to extend kind words to in a note, in person, by e-mail or text. As you follow through with this activity, pray fervently for God to deepen your love for others in the process.

6. Although kind words are deeds in themselves, sometime what we do is more important than what we say. What act or deed can you do for someone else that does not need an explanation? Know that as you practice that kind deed, few things on earth will ever feel more like heaven than what you are experiencing.

CHAPTER 11

Just Add Love

"For this very reason, make every effort to add to your faith goodness; and to goodness, knowledge; and to knowledge, self-control; and to self-control, perseverance; and to perseverance, godliness; and to godliness, brotherly kindness; and to brotherly kindness, love" (2 Peter 1:5–7).

Dr. Karl Barth, one of the most brilliant thinkers of the twentieth century, wrote volume after volume on the meaning of life and faith. After an important lecture, Dr. Barth was asked if he could summarize in one sentence all the ideas contained in those volumes. Dr. Barth thought for a moment and then said, "Jesus loves me, this I know, for the Bible tells me so."

Like Karl Barth, Peter finally got it. Peter comes right out and says, "If you possess these qualities in increasing measure, they will keep you from being ineffective and unproductive in your knowledge of our Lord Jesus Christ" (2 Peter 1:8). Peter is not a legalist; he is a realist. Peter knows the *only* way to truly "get" God's amazing love (and when I say "get" I mean "absorb it unmistakably") is to walk in the virtues of God's character. You just don't get God's love in the abstract.

Think for a moment about that beautiful exchange between Christ, Peter, and the other disciples after the Resurrection:

When they had finished breakfast, Jesus said to Simon Peter, "Simon, son of John, do you love Me more than these?" He said to Him, "Yes, Lord; You know that I love You." He said to him, "Tend My lambs." He said to him again a second time, "Simon, son of John, do you love Me?" He said to Him, "Yes, Lord; You know that I love You." He said to him, "Shepherd My sheep." He said to him the third time, "Simon, son of John, do you love Me?" Peter was grieved because He said to him the third time, "Do you love Me?" And he said to Him, "Lord, You know all things; You know that I love You." Jesus said to him, "Tend My sheep" (John 21:15–17, NASB).

After the Resurrection, Jesus engages Peter in what seems to be a painful quiz with some direct commands attached to Peter's answers. The bottom line of this interchange is that no matter what word (*phileo* or *agape*) Jesus uses to describe Peter's love for Him, Peter answers the same word (*phileo*). Perhaps Peter is still so full of self-doubt that he just can't bring himself to make any more promises about himself. Or perhaps Peter ardently loves Christ, but now knows the difference between human affection and God's love for humanity. Peter knows better than to compare the two. Either way, he obeyed Christ and became the man Christ called him to be. Ellen White observed, "The Saviour's manner of dealing with Peter had a lesson for him and his brethren. It taught them to meet the transgressor with patience, sympathy, and forgiving love. Although Peter had denied his Lord, the love which Jesus bore him never faltered. Just such love should the undershepherd feel for the sheep and lambs committed to his care. Remembering his own weakness and failure, Peter was to deal with his flock as tenderly as Christ had dealt with him."[1]

That day by the sea, Peter could not say he loved Christ the same way Christ loved the world. Such love is learned. No wonder Peter assured believers, "His divine power has given us everything we need for life and godliness" (2 Peter 1:3). It may be dormant in us, but only God's grace can bring it out of dormancy into full bloom. Furthermore, Peter urges believers to "make every effort to add" these virtues to their experience because it is the only way we will ever taste a smidgen of God's love. You can hear the stories of the Bible. You can be compelled by all manner of methods to orient your beliefs so they align with the Scripture. But ultimately, this long walk home is a learning experience in the school of God's love. If we are going to feel comfortable in our heavenly home, we must start learning about love—agape love—as we walk.

One truth of which I am certain: whatever we discover about God's love is only a fraction of the love there is to see and know. Paul hints at this in Ephesians, as he writes, "I pray that you, being rooted and established in love, may have power, together with all the saints, to grasp how wide and long and high and deep is the love of Christ, and to know this love that surpasses knowledge—that you may be filled to the measure of all the fullness of God" (3:17–19). It seems that people most deeply versed in the things of God, such as the apostles, are the ones who step back and say, "Hey. You can't fully describe or begin to exhaust God's love." Indescribable. Inexhaustible. Incomprehensible. Try it, but know that you are in over your head. Paul knew it, and he knew that the ancient prophets knew it as well. He quotes the Old Testament prophet Isaiah, claiming,

> "No eye has seen,
>   no ear has heard,
> no mind has conceived
>   what God has prepared for those who love him"—
> but God has revealed it to us by his Spirit (1 Corinthians 2:9, 10).

God's love is like the boundless ocean, the earth's unknown frontier. Scientists have discovered that most of the ocean that immediately surrounds land is approximately sixty meters deep, with rich marine life and beautiful things to see. But what we see in pictures, movies, and magazines comprises only about one-twentieth of the total ocean. But the ocean is much deeper and there is more to see. Beyond the continental shelf, the ocean drops to a depth of thirty-five hundred to six thousand meters. This is what scientists call the abyssal plain, and it is the single largest environment on earth.

The uncharted area covers more than half of the total ocean surface. But the ocean is still much deeper. In some areas of the western Pacific Ocean, the sea floor drops away into trenches with water depths of ten to eleven kilometers. We have no idea what lurks in the darkness of the ocean. Most people would not even recognize the deepest parts of the ocean. The shallow portion is beautiful and alive, but the ocean's deepest level is unlike anything most humans have ever witnessed. So is the untested, uncharted love of God.

Love embodies all virtue, but this one word can carry so many different meanings and applications: I love chocolate. I love golf. I love my sons. I love God. I love meeting new people. I love my wife Julia. When you say "I love you," you can mean so many different things. Does it mean I respect you? Does it mean I will put you first? Does it mean I would give my life for you? Love is a commitment. Love is a choice. Love is a feeling, but it is also a calling. Love tells the truth, even though it hurts. Love inspires. Love warns. Love disciplines. Love gives. Will the destruction of the wicked also be an act of love—or is it justice? And who ever dared to separate the two ideas? John said, "God is love," but that statement only continues to spin this mind-reeling circle of thought. Peter's list ends with a call to give yourself wholly to the practices that will deepen your love for God and for others.

Les Parrott, a renown author on marriage and family, notes the trouble with the word *love*, citing a thought-provoking study on college students.

"When asked, 'What makes a good marriage?' the answer given by nearly 90 percent of the population is 'Being in love.' When asked to list the essential ingredients of love as a basis for marriage, however, a survey of more than a thousand college students revealed that, 'no single item was mentioned by at least one half of those responding.' "[2]

What this research seems to say is, when we say, "I love you," it means something different to each person.

Perhaps the virtue of love is better left defined not by words, but by stories, experiences, and memories. If this is true, then maybe learning to "make every effort to add" to our faith the virtues of heaven will only communicate the meaning of love in the most beautiful, indescribable way—personification. Maybe, as we walk the road home, we discover that through belief, practice, and stories, we come to personify the meaning of the word *love,* and love becomes real. Why would that surprise us, when our best, most precise and complete definition of *love* is Jesus, the Person, as the book of Hebrews declares, "The Son is the radiance of God's glory and the exact representation of his being, sustaining all things by his powerful word" (Hebrews 1:3).

So Peter ends this beautiful cadre of virtues with love—God's love. Is no explanation necessary? The reality is more like, no explanation will cover it. Explanations tend to shortchange the beauty that comes from seeing love in action between God and people. Furthermore, since God does not walk in the flesh among us anymore, we are commissioned to carry His banner of love to all—ALL.

The New Testament is ripe with language that urges, even commands us to "love one another." John is famous for his preoccupation with how the love language of God relates to "one another." The loved apostle writes, "Beloved, let us love one another, for love is from God; and everyone who loves is born of God and knows God" (1 John 4:7, NASB). And again in his Gospel, he quotes the Savior saying, "As I have loved you, so you must love one another" (John 13:34).

While humanity seems to be searching for the meaning of love, there is a Christ who models and mirrors Heaven's perfect picture of love. As Jesus of Nazareth walked this earth, so do we. As we make our way home, let's give all our effort to discover the joy of loving others, for in that moment we experience the most basic rule of heaven.

Enough talk about love. Let's put it into practice.

Practice fellowship

We can learn the virtue of love only in community with others, which is kin to the biblical experience of fellowship. *Fellowship* simply means "spiritual partnership" that seeks to stay connected and collaborative. Dallas Willard offers this challenge to Christian connectedness: "Personalities united can contain more of God and sustain the force of his greater presence much better than scattered individuals. The fire of God kindles higher as the brands are heaped together and each is warmed by the other's flame. The members of the body must be in contact if they are to sustain and be sustained by each other."[3]

The gift of friendship is hard-wired deep inside each of us—we need to be with one another. As mentioned earlier in this chapter, the phrase "one another" or "each other" is repeated many times in the New Testament and punctuates the most difficult and perhaps greatest work of believers—togetherness. Look at just a sample of the one another/each other statements and imagine what might change in your community of faith if these promptings were obeyed.

- "Be at peace with each other" (Mark 9:50).
- Be devoted to one another. . . . Honor one another (Romans 12:10).
- Live in harmony with one another (Romans 12:16).
- Therefore let us stop passing judgment on one another (Romans 14:13).
- Accept one another (Romans 15:7).
- Instruct one another (Romans 15:14).
- Serve one another in love (Galatians 5:13).

• Be kind and compassionate to one another, forgiving each other, just as in Christ God forgave you (Ephesians 4:32).

Some are clearly more challenging than others. But crowd them together under one roof, and what you have is a family. It's kind of scary in a way, but nothing is more natural than home, which, by the way, is where we are headed. It is my sneaking suspicion that the more we practice Christian fellowship, the more we will discover the coves and caves and uncharted realms of God's love. So choose someone to accept that is outside your circle. Examine your heart and identify a fellow believer, neighbor, or coworker to whom you might extend mercy by suspending your criticism. Perhaps there is someone you feel compelled to instruct or serve or even forgive. The field is open—and there is a lot to learn.

Practice sacrifice

Jesus seemingly identified love's highest achievement when He stated, "Greater love has no one than this, that he lay down his life for his friends" (John 15:13). But the real question is, Who are my friends? Are our friends the ones who reciprocate our affinity, loyalty, and interests? If that is the case, Jesus had very few friends. What if Jesus defined *friend* as "anyone you choose to befriend, regardless of that person's response to you"? Let me give you an example.

Reading Marcus Luttrell's *Lone Survivor,*[4] I find my worldview expanded by the story of four navy SEALs sent to Afghanistan in 2005. The handful of soldiers were inserted on a high mountain range near the border of Pakistan. Their mission was to capture or take out a high-ranking Taliban leader. While the SEALs were doing reconnaissance, a couple of Afghan goatherds happened upon them. The soldiers faced a dilemma. Even though they didn't want to kill civilians, the probability was high that the herders would report the SEALs' presence to the Taliban.

The soldiers let the locals go, and within a brief time, they were attacked by more than one hundred Taliban solders.

Lt. Michael Murphy, the commander, was killed while trying to call for backup. Two other soldiers, Matthew Axelson and Daniel Dietz, were killed in the attack. Marcus Luttrell escaped the storm of bullets by tumbling down the mountainside, breaking a vertebrae, sustaining a gunshot wound in his leg, and suffering various cuts and contusions. For two days, he evaded the enemy until a group of Afghan villagers found him getting a drink of water from a nearby stream. When the Pashtun villagers found him, they took him in and offered him *lokhay*. The Pashtun tribe obeys a two-thousand-year-old code of hospitality. To extend *lokhay* to another is to assimilate that person into your village and protect him with your life if need be. The Taliban soldiers surrounded the village, and the local Pashtun people almost lost their lives in defense of this stranger who in a moment became a member, a friend. Eventually, Marcus Luttrell was rescued by Green Berets and airlifted out, but the story blows apart this notion that Christian believers have exclusive rights to the idea of Godlike love.

I have no idea whether the Pashtun villagers had ever heard of Jesus or His call to lay down your life for your friend, but what this story means is both unsettling and inspiring. Let's summarize it. In the middle of a war of competing, hostile values, a small group of Afghans risked their lives to save an American soldier. Friendship is not always mutual affinity or even a reciprocated commitment. It is a choice to befriend. It is an act of grace. It is the very essence of what Christ did for humanity, and what He calls His followers to do for others.

This kind of befriending calls for sacrifice. It calls you to give up your position, your advantage, and even your life. It is a leap of faith, a risk taken that makes you vulnerable. Even writing these words I'm so convicted by the enormity of what it might mean. All of the logical excuses I think of as to why this kind of love is crazy and untenable today are like wisps of smoke vanishing into thin air. The arguments simply don't hold. This is by far the hardest thing Christ has ever required of His disciples. But it is the one quality that distinguishes whom you belong to and where you are going. "By this all men will know that you are my disciples, if you love one another" (John 13:35).

While most of you reading this are not in a war zone, you are in a place where you can befriend someone who needs a friend like Jesus. It is likely that you will experience the love that Peter calls us to add to our lives as you extend your friendship to someone who will be changed by it. But even more, the exercise may begin to liberate us all from the urge to choose self-preservation as our first response. I think William Barclay explained it well: "Christianity does not think of a man finally submitting to the power of God; it thinks of him as finally surrendering to the love of God. It is not that man's will is crushed, but that man's heart is broken."[5]

As we make our way home, the virtues of God's character are before us to practice, put on, and flesh out. This is the messiest endeavor of all because we teeter between the human and the divine, between our will versus God's, but we ultimately stir up good things in our nature that uproot some unattractive qualities at the same time. When I practice brotherly kindness, but my action is thrown back in my face or misunderstood, I can't help but react, sometimes even by ignoring everything I had previously learned about self-control. In such situations, be reminded and refreshed by Peter's words: "If you possess these qualities in increasing measure, they will keep you from being ineffective and unproductive in your knowledge of our Lord Jesus Christ. But if anyone does not have them, he is nearsighted and blind, and has forgotten that he has been cleansed from his past sins" (2 Peter 1:8, 9). Please don't miss this. If you struggle, don't give up or go away, but go back to Calvary, where we started. The Cross reminds us that sin is real and that God's grace is victorious. At the Cross, we are adopted into Christ's family and are called to make our way home. If you find yourself floundering and failing, get back to Calvary and remind yourself about the way home. The hymn "At the Cross" is playing through my mind, and my heart is glad.

> Alas! And did my Savior bleed
> And did my Sovereign die?
> Would He devote that sacred head
> For sinners such as I?

> At the cross, at the cross where I first saw the light,
> And the burden of my heart rolled away,
> It was there by faith I received my sight,
> And now I am happy all the day!

> Was it for crimes that I had done
> He groaned upon the tree?
> Amazing pity! grace unknown!
> And love beyond degree!

> Well might the sun in darkness hide
> And shut His glories in,
> When Christ, the mighty Maker died,
> For man the creature's sin.

> Thus might I hide my blushing face
> While Calv'ry's cross appears,
> Dissolve my heart in thankfulness
> And melt mine eyes to tears.

> But drops of grief can ne'er repay
> The debt of love I owe:
> Here, Lord, I give myself away
> 'Tis all that I can do![6]

1. Ellen G. White, *The Desire of Ages* (Nampa, Idaho: Pacific Press® Publishing Association, 1940), 815.

2. Les and Leslie Parrott, *Saving Your Second Marriage Before It Starts: Nine Questions to Ask Before (and After) You Remarry* (Grand Rapids, Mich.: Zondervan, 2001), 53.

3. Dallas Willard, *The Spirit of the Disciplines: Understanding How God Changes Lives* (New York: Harper Collins, 1991), 186, 187.

4. Marcus Luttrell, *Lone Survivor* (New York: Little, Brown and Company, 2007).

5. William Barclay, *New Testament Words* (Louisville, Ky.: Westminster John Knox Press, 1974), 23.

6. Isaac Watts and Ralph Hudson, "At the Cross."

Questions for Reflection

1. Replay in your mind the song "Jesus Loves Me." Then explain why you think that song is timelessly profound.

2. In what way is the word *love* hard to define but easier to show or describe in action?

3. Replay in your mind the scene with Peter and Jesus by the Sea of Galilee after the Resurrection. Try to imagine what Peter was going through. Why do you think Jesus pushed Peter so hard?

4. Of all the Bible passages mentioned in this chapter, which do you resonate with? Which action of Christian love do you find to be most difficult? Why?

5. Review the story of Marcus Luttrell in Afghanistan. When have you learned about love, community, and grace from an unsuspected source?

6. With whom can you practice a "befriending" spirit this week?

Part 3: Storify How You Came to Make Your Way Home

By trade he was a tinker, a man who made and mended pots and pans. Ordinary people with such humble trades typically go unnoticed in the timeline of history—except this man told a story, the story of the human struggle of making your way home. John Bunyan's life is a roller-coaster ride of repeated tragedy, disappointment, and personal failure, mixed with his passionate devotion to preaching the gospel and sorting out the truth as revealed in Scripture. For a hundred years after it was published, his book *Pilgrim's Progress* remained immensely popular, second only to the Bible.

Bunyan's conversion to Christ consisted of a long process rather than any one event or specific point in time. It has been noted that Bunyan's conversion "was neither smooth nor straight. He struggled with assurance of salvation, his daughter's blindness, poverty, his wife's death, and his desire to preach the gospel when it was forbidden by law."[1] *Pilgrim's Progress* is really a story about "the Story"—the journey of humanity to answer the question "What must I do to be saved?" It seems that some of the most powerful writings come from authors writing in prison cells. Bunyan wrote the infamous story of "Christian" in two parts over the course of two different imprisonments. The enduring value of this allegory is the way it honestly and vividly reminds humanity of the story—

the human story of God and people. Paul Bunyan's contribution to the Christian journey is simply monumental. What we remember when we read *Pilgrim's Progress* is that the walk home demands a deliberate choice to focus on the destination.[2]

For those of us who are making our way home, we must pay attention to the story, or we might forget where we are going, not to mention why we are headed for that particular destination.

Somewhere between "once upon a time" and "they lived happily ever after," we live out our part of one true story. I love pictorial timelines that portray key stories in human history. I imagine what my picture would look like on such a mural. *What were these ancient heroes of faith like? Were they really as ordinary as I am?*

The Christian walk home doesn't seem to make sense without a vision of the story in which we have a part. Luke's Gospel captures our unbroken storyline in this genealogy, "When He began His ministry, Jesus Himself was about thirty years of age, being, as was supposed, the son of Joseph, the son of Eli . . . the son of Noah, the son of Lamech, the son of Methuselah, the son of Enoch, the son of Jared, the son of Mahalaleel, the son of Cainan, the son of Enosh, the son of Seth, the son of Adam, the son of God" (Luke 3:23–38, NASB).

From the time of Jesus back to the beginning of time, everyone is linked together to one relationship—Adam and Eve, the sons and daughters of God. We are all part of one true story. Most people agree that stories are the most profound teaching tool as well as the most memorable. For example, choose one of your favorite movies: You could probably retrace almost every scene. You know the moral or truth the story tries to convey. The images may never leave your mind. Stories are powerful.

Stories are also powerful communicators of ideas. Ivan Illich, an Austrian philosopher and anarchist, was once asked how to change society. This was his reply: "Neither revolution nor reformation can ultimately change a society. Rather, you must tell a new powerful tale, one so persuasive that it sweeps away the old myths and becomes the preferred story. If you want to change a society, then you have to tell an alternative story."[3]

Eugene Peterson observed, "We live in a world impoverished of story. Words in our culture are a form of currency used mostly to provide information. Contemporary schooling is primarily an exercise in piling up information. By the time we have completed our assigned years in the classroom, we have far more information than we will ever be able to put to use."[4]

Peter knew the power of stories; as a Jew he was raised on the storied promise of the children of God and the hope of Israel's Messiah. Every year of his life, Peter witnessed firsthand the festivals, which were essentially about reliving the acts of God in history. Long before the pen or keyboard, there was the story and the memory. The stories of Genesis are known today only because people committed the events to memory and systematically repeated them so they might endure.

Peter committed the words and works of the Savior to memory and narrated while Mark penned the story. Peter's portrait of Jesus is really a fast-paced series of stories told around the campfire. The word *immediately* introduces almost every major incident, and Peter tends to speak with passionate, emotional language. Peter knew the power of stories, for good or evil. Near the end of his journey, he made the following remark about evil storytellers: "In their greed these teachers will exploit you with stories they have made up" (2 Peter 2:3). He contrasts his own stories to those of the false teachers: "We did not follow cleverly invented stories when we told you about the power and coming of our Lord Jesus Christ, but we were eyewitnesses of his majesty" (2 Peter 1:16).

Eyewitnesses. Firsthand experience. Peter's claim goes far beyond simply bearing witness to Christ; he steps into the storied life of all who have made their way home. We need stories to be reminded that we are called to be holy. The word *holy* "denotes that which is 'sanctified' or 'set apart' for divine service."⁵ This final section fleshes out what it means to be holy, to be a saint. Fortunately, the true meaning is far different from the stereotype of a flawless person with a nimbus of light circling his or her head. Listen to how Peter encourages the saints; try to see what makes them holy.

If you possess these qualities in increasing measure, they will keep you from being ineffective and unproductive in your knowledge of our Lord Jesus Christ. But if anyone does not have them, he is nearsighted and blind, and has forgotten that he has been cleansed from his past sins. Therefore, my brothers, be all the more eager to make your calling and election sure. For if you do these things, you will never fall, and you will receive a rich welcome into the eternal kingdom of our Lord and Savior Jesus Christ. So I will always remind you of these things, even though you know them and are firmly established in the truth you now have. I think it is right to refresh your memory as long as I live in the tent of this body, because I know that I will soon put it aside, as our Lord Jesus Christ has made clear to me. And I will make every effort to see that after my departure you will always be able to remember these things (2 Peter 1:8–15).

At least two truths emerge from this passage to shape our idea of holiness:

1. Storifying paints a wide-angled picture of the meaning of our journey home. If we are not growing or don't feel at peace with God, it is because we forgotten about Calvary. If we are off track, we needn't blame our feet; instead, we must blame our eyes. Peter says, "You have forgotten that your sins were forgiven." We forget or don't see the way ahead clearly because, as Peter says, we are "nearsighted and blind." It's true. The times when my own walk with God seemed disoriented and futile, what I needed most was perspective, to step back to see the bigger picture. Nothing colors the canvas of our lives like stories that reveal the big picture. And no event so stands out on the mural of human life as Calvary. At the Cross, we see who God is and who we are. We see how we are bound to God. We see the event of the Resurrection and witness firsthand that God is working His plan to bring us home. What a story!

2. Storifying enables us to remember. Remembering our purpose and our destination is essential because it separates us from the world and devotes us to our journey home with Christ. For this we need to tell our stories. The best sermons, the best books, songs, and meaningful events in our lives are bound by one core element—the narrative.

Peter is fully aware of his earlier disloyalty. But he tells these stories anyway because "whatever was written in earlier times was written for our instruction, so that through perseverance and the encouragement of the Scriptures we might have hope" (Romans 15:4, NASB).

Hope. Hope is the theme of our metanarrative. Hope is the hallmark of our one true story. Hope is the salient message of the ancient Exodus, which is why the storytellers of the Old and New Testaments remind us constantly that we are pilgrims on our walk home. The storied journey continues today for the saints—yes, as Peter would say, "that includes you." But you must learn to enter into the story of your brothers and sisters of long ago and walk with them, remembering your ultimate destination.

---

1. E. Michael and Sharon Rusten, *The One Year Book of Christian History* (Wheaton, Ill.: Tyndale House Publishers, 2003), 98.

2. Ibid.

3. Tony Dale, Felicity Dale, and George Barna, *The Rabbit and the Elephant: Why Small Is the New Big for Today's Church* (Carol Stream, Ill.: BarnaBooks, 2009), 133.

4. Eugene Peterson, *Stories of Jesus* (Colorado Springs, Colo.: NavPress, 1999), 8.

5. *Nelson's Illustrated Bible Dictionary*, 1986 ed., s.v. "holy."

CHAPTER 12

Peter's Final Reminder

If you possess these qualities in increasing measure, they will keep you from being ineffective and unproductive in your knowledge of our Lord Jesus Christ. But if anyone does not have them, he is nearsighted and blind, and has *forgotten* that he has been cleansed from his past sins.

Therefore, my brothers, be all the more eager to make your calling and election sure. For if you do these things, you will never fall, and you will receive a rich welcome into the eternal kingdom of our Lord and Savior Jesus Christ.

So I will always *remind* you of these things, even though you know them and are firmly established in the truth you now have. I think it is right to *refresh your memory* as long as I live in *the tent of this body,* because I know that I will soon put it aside, as our Lord Jesus Christ has made clear to me. And I will make every effort to see that after my *departure* you will always be able to *remember* these things.

We did not follow cleverly invented stories when we told you about the power and coming of our Lord Jesus Christ, but we were *eyewitnesses* of his majesty. For he received honor and glory from God the Father when the voice came to him from the Majestic

Glory, saying, "This is my Son, whom I love; with him I am well pleased." We ourselves heard this voice that came from heaven when we were with him on the sacred mountain (2 Peter 1:8–18; emphasis added).

Peter surprises me. Early on we typecast Peter unfairly as a nonthinking, fight-first kind of guy. A man's man. A fisherman—rugged and simple, but always ready to go. Perhaps Peter has been misunderstood. It happens. Alan, a friend and colaborer of mine introduced me at a university assembly by offering publicly his first impressions of me saying, "When I first met Pastor Troy, I judged him prematurely to be a 'dumb jock.' It turns out that he is not as athletic as I first thought." Touché! Take a deep, long look at Peter's life, journey, and especially his letter—his last will and testament to the church, and it is clear Peter is no "dumb jock." Peter is truly an apostle par excellence.

The following chapters are the very treasure of my heart and hope for my church. But in order for them to ring coherently, I want to unpack this passage in a similar manner as in the beginning of this book. The words and phrases italicized are key to understanding the reason we must learn to storify.

Peter uses five themes that capture his desire to lead the precious flock of believers safely home: (1) living in a *tent,* (2) Peter's *exodus,* (3) being re-mindful, (4) the glorious appearing, and (5) the Christian eyewitness. So Peter, after reminding the believers about starting the walk home because of God's grace in Christ (2 Peter 1:2–4), and after encouraging them to experience the virtues of God's eternal home (verses 5–7), now tells them how to arrive home (verses 8–18).

Living in a tent

When Peter asserts, "As long as I live in the tent of this body," he is connecting his walk on earth to the journey of the ancients. Peter sees himself a sojourner, a traveler who is making his way home. To refer to his body as a tent is to identify with Abraham, Isaac, and Jacob—and especially with the children of Israel. Peter lives in a tent because this world is not his home—he is only on a camping trip. Peter has no permanent plans for life on earth. His direction is fixed and his way is clear.

William Barclay agrees, saying this about the tent: "This was a favourite picture with the early Christian writers. . . . The picture comes from the journeyings of the patriarchs in the Old Testament. They had no abiding residence but lived in tents because they were on the way to the Promised Land. The Christian knows well that his life in this world is not a permanent residence but a journey towards the world beyond."[1]

At every funeral I officiate or attend, I hear myself say, "I just want to go home." Whether you are young or simply young at heart, after you spend enough time on earth, the mansions and monuments become petty, and the desire for heaven intensifies. Peter says, "This is a good thing."

Peter's exodus

A second theme on Peter's mind in his final moments is about his final moments. Shocking. Peter said to the flock, "I will make every effort to see that after my departure . . ." (verse 15). Do you ever get uncomfortable when old people, or even not-so-old people, talk about their death—their departure? (Even more awkward is when your family and friends are talking about your *departure* more than you are, but that is another discussion.) The word Peter uses for departure is critical: the word for departure is the word *exodus*. Peter is not hyperfocused about dying as he is enamored with the notion of the exciting departure for the Promised Land. Oh, don't miss the distinction—because it is huge! It's not death Peter longs for; it is home.

Imagine knowing what is to come. The Roman soldiers with their clanging iron armor will soon march Peter to his own Calvary. He will be tortured and flogged in the same manner as Christ. He will be nailed to a cross in a different manner, however, because He is not the Lord. He is only learning to love (*agape*) like Jesus. Peter's imminent death is not payment for anyone's debt, especially not his own. Peter's debt has been paid in full by Jesus. Jesus was the Promise of God; and Peter, although considered a fool for believing such a "silly" story, faces his final moments of physical agony. But his physical pain pales compared to the way he aches for home. It is almost as if Peter, as he looks ahead to his own crucifixion, does not see the whip, the nails, the wood, or the blood. Peter sees the stars under the open sky on the outskirts of Egypt. He feels the sand between his toes and the vast possibilities of life without chains and a world with no boundaries. His imminent death is, by his own profession, his exit out of Egypt toward the Promised Land. Now, can you see how people were able to suffer but still confess Christ?

One more thought about Peter's exodus. Jesus promised Peter by the sea: " 'I tell you the truth, when you were younger you dressed yourself and went where you wanted; but when you are old you will stretch out your hands, and someone else will dress you and lead you where you do not want to go.' Jesus said this to indicate the kind of death by which Peter would glorify God. Then he said to him, 'Follow me!' " (John 21:18, 19).

After reinstating Peter, by encouraging him to learn to love through imitating Christ's work on earth, Jesus tells Peter how he will die. Here is my sanctified-imagination paraphrase of what Jesus said to Peter:

Follow Me, Peter—not in the way you imagined when I first called you by the sea. You thought that you would be a player in bringing down Rome and that Israel would be glorified. You will not follow Me in that way. It will not be anything like you were thinking when you were arguing with John about who was going to be the most honored apostle in My cabinet. It's not going to end like that. Peter, do you remember the time I told you how I would die? Yes. I called you the mouthpiece of Satan. How could you forget? The one thing you couldn't stomach was how I would die, but I have news for you, Peter. You, too, will embrace a cross. They will stretch you out like they did Me, but unlike Me, it won't hurt like hell. I tasted hell once and for all. This is not your hell; in fact, you will feel as if you are going home. So, knowing what you know now, Peter, follow Me.

That question is for us as well, now that we know where all of this is going. Do you follow? You may have said Yes to Jesus before, but did you really know what you were signing up for? Perhaps you did. But if you didn't, each new day provides you with the opportunity to start your walk home—with full disclosure of all you need to know about the journey and the destination. My prayer is that you will choose to join Peter, and to follow.

Being re-mindful

Four times in this section Peter nudges us about the need to remember, to not forget, or not to forget about remembering.

- Has forgotten (2 Peter 1:9).
- I will always remind you (verse 12).
- It is right to refresh your memory (verse 13).
- You will always be able to remember (verse 15).

Peter knows that, historically, the problem for believers is forgetting. The blindness, the shortsightedness, the temptation to forget and fall away is so real to Peter. No one became a follower of Christ without first hearing the story. Peter makes it clear; "These aren't little sugar-stick stories created or fabricated to get you on board." The storied lives of believers from Adam and Eve to us today ring with the truth of one true story that makes our experience meaningful. We won't forget unless we fail to tell the story.

The glorious appearing

The chief theme in Peter's last words to the people includes a reference to the second coming of Christ: "We did not follow cleverly invented stories when we told you about the power and coming of our Lord Jesus Christ, but we were eyewitnesses of his majesty" (verse 16). Peter seems almost defensive, but the Second Coming is a common theme of the New Testament church. What is more surprising is Peter's allusion to the transfiguration of Jesus. It is as though Peter is saying, "I can talk of the reality of the second coming of Christ because I was there on the mount when Jesus was transfigured. And, friends, let me tell you, the resurrection of the saints—it's real."

Why? The Transfiguration is connected with the second coming of Christ and the resurrection of the dead by two things: style and context. The style of the Transfiguration and the presence of humans who have tasted death and are now alive (Moses) and those who have not tasted death (Elijah) show up in a shiny, loud, glorious display. The context of all three Transfiguration stories is preceded by Jesus saying, "The Son of Man is going to come in his Father's glory with his angels, and then he will reward each person according to what he has done. I tell you the truth, some who are standing here will not taste death before they see the Son of Man coming in his kingdom" (Matthew 16:27, 28; see also Mark 9:1; Luke 9:26, 27).

Peter testifies, almost as if he is in court, saying, "He is coming. I know. I was there on the mountain. I saw the glory of heaven. I personally witnessed Moses and Elijah. I heard the voice of God and I know He will return. Be ready!"

The Christian eyewitness

Peter ties up this final section up with the statement, "We were eye-witnesses of his majesty" (2 Peter 1:16). The word translated eyewitness is *epoptes,* which means an overseer, a spectator, one who has seen something firsthand. It was applied especially to a select group of people who were able to witness a passion play so powerful that being there connected them with others who were there and experienced the same. Peter claims that "we were eyewitnesses." Remember his beautiful words of encouragement in 1 Peter?

> In this you greatly rejoice, though now for a little while you may have had to suffer grief in all kinds of trials. These have come so that your faith—of greater worth than gold, which perishes even though refined by fire—may be proved genuine and may result in praise, glory and honor when Jesus Christ is revealed. Though you have not seen him, you love him; and even though you do not see him now, you believe in him and are filled with an inexpressible and glorious joy, for you are receiving the goal of your faith, the salvation of your souls (1 Peter 1:6–9).

These are themes of Peter's final moments. We must find ways to storify our journey home as we temporarily live in a tent. We storify our own exodus because if we don't, we forget. We may not forget all the little points and truths about life, but we will miss *the point* and *the truth* in *the Person of Christ* if we fail to storify our journey home. We must ultimately storify our experience because it is the only way others will hear and join the glorious walk home.

---

1. William Barclay, *The Letters of James and Peter,* 308.

Questions for Reflection

1. When have you had to live in a transition stage? Were you patient and long-suffering about the little things because you knew it wouldn't always be that way? How is the journey of the Christian life like living in a tent?

2. Two things happened to Israel in the Exodus (1) they were set on a journey to another land and another way of life, and (2) they struggled to keep their destination before them. In what way are we, along with Peter, in our own exodus?

3. In this chapter, Peter clearly tries to warn people to avoid the shipwreck of forgetting where they are going. How do you remind yourself of the things that are most important?

4. How would you say the Transfiguration relates to the second coming of Jesus? What was the purpose and how did the event affect Peter?

5. In 1 Peter 1:6–9, the apostle acknowledges that most people who believe never see Christ in person. How is this passage an encouragement to you and others who travel home by faith?

6. In what way do believers today have more information than even those who saw Christ in person?

CHAPTER 13

Putting the I in Redeemed

Max Lucado, in *And The Angels Were Silent,* tells the story of a walk eighty-year-old Mary Barbour claims she will never forget.

One of the first things that I remembers was my pappy waking me up in the middle of the night, dressing me in the dark, all the time telling me to be quiet. One of the twins hollered some and Pappy put his hand over its mouth to keep quiet.

After we dressed, he went outside and peeped around for a minute, then he comed back in and got us. We snook out of the house and along the woods path, Pappy toting one of the twins and holding me by the hand and Mammy carrying the other two.

I reckons I will always remember that walk, with the bushes slapping my legs, the wind sighing in the trees, and the hoot owls and the whippoorwills hollering at each other from the big trees. I was half asleep and scared stiff, but in a little while we pass the plum thicket and there am the mules and the wagon. There am the quilt in the bottom of the wagon, and on this they lays we younguns. And Pappy and Mammy gets on the board across the front and drives off down the road.

I was sleepy, but I was scared too, so as we rides along, I listens to Pappy and Mammy talk. Pappy was telling Mammy about the Yankees coming to their plantation, burning the corncribs, the smokehouses and destroying everything. He says right low that they done took Marster Jordan to the rip raps down nigh Norfolk, and that he stole the mules and the wagon and escaped.[1]

Seventy years later, Mary Barbour said, "I reckons I will always remember that walk."

Peter keenly felt the exodus—that walk to freedom. Born in the knowledge of his crucified and risen Lord, he walked from slavery to sin to the freedom that comes from walking home. Whenever I'm on a plane and hear the attendant say, "Look for the exit closest to you," I smile and think of Peter. If we are to experience this walk ourselves and become eyewitnesses to His majesty, we should briefly look in Scripture for the exits close to us. Doing this will enable us to put ourselves into the story of the redeemed who are on the journey to the Promised Land.

Yousuf Karsh was a Canadian portrait photographer who spent fifty years taking pictures of some of the most famous people of the twentieth century. The only picture he took of someone's back was of Pablo Casals in a small French abbey in 1954.

As Karsh was setting up his equipment, Casals began playing Bach on his cello. As if transported to another place and time, Karsh was so enthralled by the music that he almost forgot why he was there. In that moment, Karsh caught the picture of a stooped, bald-headed man bent over his cello, frozen in time against the aged stone of the chapel wall. When the portrait was on exhibition in the Museum of Fine Arts in Boston, the curator noticed another bald-headed, elderly man who came day after day and stood silently in front of the photograph for long periods of time. Finally, the curator tapped the old man on the shoulder and asked him what he was doing. With obvious irritation, the old man turned to the curator and said, "Hush, young man! Can't you see I'm listening to the music?"

When has a picture or a piece of music transported you to another place and time—where you felt as if you were actually there? It is amazing how a story can have the power to launch your mind to another place, to make you feel as if you actually were there.

During the 1950s, CBS aired a Sunday night program called *You Are There.* The format was a news program with actors portraying scenes from history as if they were recent events. The angle of the cameras, the mob of reporters seemed to transport the audience to the moment during which they became a part of history. The subjects focused on people such as Galileo and Joan of Arc, whose stories were vehicles for discussions about intellectual and political freedom. One of the nasty little secrets about this program is that all of the writers were included on the McCarthy-era blacklist—a group of people who were labeled as un-American because of their real or supposed sympathy with Communist ideology.

More important than stories making history come alive to make a political point is the ability of stories to make a spiritual connection. We want our children, grandchildren, and every generation to love God with their hearts, souls, and strength. How can we ensure that each generation will become believers who are headed for home? Consider the advice given by Moses to the children of Israel on the brink of entering into the Promised Land: "Hear, O Israel: The LORD our God, the LORD is one. Love the LORD your God with all your heart and with all your soul and with all your strength. These commandments that I give you today are to be upon your hearts. Impress them on your children. Talk about them when you sit at home and when you walk along the road, when you lie down and when you get up. Tie them as symbols on your hands and bind them on your foreheads. Write them on the doorframes of your houses and on your gates" (Deuteronomy 6:4–9).

Moses reminded the people that the story of their deliverance must not be lost in the drama of the day or in the struggle of getting to the Promised Land. The aged prophet knew that if the Israelites did not integrate the significance of their deliverance in a real, meaningful way, they would once again lose their identity and their mission. And so these words are to be upon hearts—in a way that no one can dismiss, with clarity, meaning, and conviction. And as you can read, not just once a week or occasionally when you have time, always be thinking about how you can communicate the truth about how you have been set free from sin to follow the Lord. This storifying mind-set is echoed in the music that Asaph wrote in the Psalms. Notice the passion for telling the story to the next generation:

O my people, hear my teaching;
    listen to the words of my mouth.
I will open my mouth in parables
    I will utter hidden things, things from of old—
what we have heard and known
    what our fathers have told us.
We will not hide them from their children
    we will tell the next generation
the praiseworthy deeds of the LORD,
    his power, and the wonders he has done.
He decreed statutes for Jacob
    and established the law in Israel,
which he commanded our forefathers
    to teach their children,
so the next generation would know them,
    even the children yet to be born,
    and they in turn would tell their children (Psalm 78:1–6).

What I appreciate about Asaph's song is that he takes personal responsibility for passing the story of the Exodus and the Promised Land to the next generation. When you find your place in the grand narrative of going home, you want to tell the story in a way that invites others also to make their way home.

For the church today, we find ourselves perplexed by many things. But if we sift through our stuff, we are left with one objective—to find a way to teach others how to experience the reality of being a child of God and of deliverance from sin. And while the method is offered in Deuteronomy 6, there is more to the task of passing the torch of faith than simply telling the next generation what to think and do. The goal was to keep the story of grace before them, day and night, all the time—on the doorposts, on bumper stickers and T-shirts, every possible venue to communicate truth was and is to be used! Some might reply, "We are already doing all of that. We are teaching, we have classes and programs and textbooks and vespers and . . ." But simply peppering people with facts might fill them with information—but, as you will see, we need something else for them to experience the transformation. Most people stop reading after the "love the Lord your God" part of this passage— what else is there? Later on in the passage, the cagey old prophet unveils the secret weapon for binding people to God.

In Deuteronomy 6:20–23, Moses extends the lesson to the inevitable questions that come from children as they mature into adolescence: "In the future, when your son asks you, 'What is the meaning of the stipulations, decrees and laws the LORD our God has commanded you?' tell him: 'We were slaves of Pharaoh in Egypt, but the LORD brought us out of Egypt with a mighty hand. Before our eyes the LORD sent miraculous signs and wonders—great and terrible—upon Egypt and Pharaoh and his whole household. But he brought us out from there to bring us in and give us the land that he promised on oath to our forefathers.' "

Believe me, they will ask. Their inquiry is about meaning. Why? What is the meaning of all of these dos and don'ts. When they ask that about the significance of the Sabbath, the answer is not, "Because it's the Sabbath!" or "Because the Bible says so!" But the secret weapon is "Because I was a slave in Egypt, and the God who created me, delivered me with a mighty hand and gave me this day to remember that I am His." The most salient truth emerging from Moses on how to pass on the faith is the command to tell the story of the Exodus, the glorious journey where slaves become free. We can memorize the list of commands and raise our hands in agreement a set of beliefs, but those parts cease to be *the truth* until seen against the backdrop of the story. Much like the story of the little boy who probably believed his mother loved him, but never really knew the story.

A story is told of a young boy who asked his mom if she would go with him to his first teacher-parent conference. She agreed, but was surprised and a little embarrassed. Although his mother was beautiful, her face bore a scar across one side. It was at the conference that his teacher and all his classmates first saw his mother, and he didn't know what to do or what people would think of his mom because of her terrible scar. He withdrew into the corner and tried to hide from the others but still see what was going one. He was close enough to see, and, more important, close enough to hear what happened next.

His teacher introduced herself, and with kind honesty, inquired how the mother's face had become scarred. The little boy leaned into the conversation from the corner because he never heard the story about how his mother's face had been injured.

"When my son was a baby," the mother replied, "he was in a room that caught on fire. Everyone was afraid to go in because the fire was out of control, so I went in. As I was running toward his crib, I saw a beam falling and I placed myself over him to shield him. I was knocked unconscious but fortunately, a fireman came in and saved both of us. The scar is permanent but to this day, I have never regretted doing what I did."

On hearing what his mother did for him, the little boy leapt out of hiding place and threw his arms around her. All of the facts and truths fell into one beautiful place, and he would never be embarrassed by that scar again. In fact, it could be the one story he would tell all his life.[2] Perhaps our greatest task as believers is learning to put the *I* in "redeemed." *I* was there. It happened to *me. I'm* one of the ones—the saints, who live and walk the trail home. So, we start by storytelling. Consider the three aspects of telling the story.

Tell *the story*

Again, there is one story that runs through the whole of Scripture and the center of our lives—the storied relationship between God and people. This is what we call a metanarrative—a story that explains all the little stories of our lives. In fact, stories are what connect humanity from the beginning of time. Stories reveal, awaken, inspire, and define the truth with greater impact than any list or theoretical abstractions.

Do you have a family member who, no matter how often you may have heard it, tells the same story over and over with almost irritating passion? Do you have stories that anchor your soul and give you a sense of purpose in life?

Tell the story *as though you were there*

But there is more to this than just telling the story—the counsel from Moses was quite clear. When your children ask, tell the story *as though you were there*. What makes this counsel so amazing is the audience. Who is the book of Deuteronomy written to? It is written to the people who were born in the desert; they had never set foot in Egypt; they didn't know Pharaoh or anything about the night of the Passover. They are the children of those who had been delivered. And God's challenge is for you to tell your children—I was a slave in Egypt, God brought *me* out. The second-generation Israelites had never lived in Egypt, but they are told to tell the story *as though they were there.*

Tell your story *because you were there*

They only way new generations will experience faith is for them to find a way to connect their story with the great, grand narrative that reaches into their future. Every new generation places their struggle with sin and grace and love of devotion, their quest for meaning, and their deep burden to give, their desire to know more—within the metanarrative. When the new generation can rest their lives, their walk, their own seemingly simple storied journey safely in the great story of God's narrative of redemption, then and only then does their faith experience mature.

Extending the flame from one generation to the next

In the early days of the Tennessee Valley Project, a dilapidated log homestead had to be abandoned to make room for a lake behind the dam. A new home on the hillside had already been erected for the cabin's poor Appalachian family, but they refused to move into their beautiful new split-level ranch ("splanch" they called it).

The day of the flooding arrived, but still the family refused to move. As the bulldozers were brought in, the Appalachian family brought out their shotguns. No amount of legal brandishing or bulldozer menacing would budge this family from their cabin. Then someone from the TVA decided to try one last-ditch effort to end the stalemate. They called in a social worker to talk with the family and find out what their problem was.

"We ain't goin' anywhere," the family announced to the social worker. "Nobody can make us. We're not budging no matter how many threats you make or how rundown our li'l cabin may look to you!"

The social worker pleaded, "Help me to explain to the authorities why you won't move into your beautiful new home."

"See that fire over there?" the man asked, pointing to a blazing fire in the primitive hearth of the log cottage. "My grandpa built that fire over a hundred years ago," the man explained. "He never let it go out, for he had no matches and it was a long way to a neighbor's. Then my pa tended the fire, and since he died, I've tended it. None of us ever let it die, and I ain't a-goin' to move away now and let Grandpa's fire go out!"

This gave the social worker an idea. She arranged for a large apple butter kettle to be delivered to the home. She explained to the family that they could scoop up the live coals from the fire and carry them to the new house, where they would then be poured out and fresh kindling added. In this way Grandpa's fire need never go out. Would this be acceptable? This Appalachian family huddled, and then agreed under those conditions to move from their shack in the hollow up to the new home on the hillside.

All of their belongings were moved, but they never let the kettle with the burning coals out of their sight. The family wouldn't budge until they could take with them the fire of their ancestors.

Before there were fundamental beliefs, there was a once-upon-a-time where sin invaded the hearts of humankind. Beneath the corruption and shame, a desire for freedom and a yearning for purpose stirred the hopes of God's children on earth. Besides all the truths humanity wrestles with, there is one truth revealed in the story of redemption: "You are free to walk home." Beyond our shortsighted steps on earth is a vision of unspeakable of glory and rest for our sore feet. Behind every pilgrim walking this road today are brothers and sisters like Moses and Peter and Mary, who identify with every step we take today. Because Christ delivered on His promise at Calvary, believe Him, enter into the story, the one true story that endures in every generation.

1. Max Lucado, *And The Angels Were Silent: Walking With Christ Toward the Cross* (Colorado Springs, Colo.: Multnomah Books, 1999).

2. Adapted from Lih Yuh Kuo, "The Scar," *A 4th Course of Chicken Soup for the Soul* (Deerfield Beach, Fla.: HCI Books, 1997).

Questions for Reflection

1. Who are the storytellers in your family? What stories have you heard over and over again?

2. If you had to tell three stories that shaped your life the most, which stories would you tell? What would be your exodus story—the testimony of when you were redeemed?

3. Imagine being a participant in the Exodus and leaving the confines of Egypt. What do you think freedom felt like?

4. For centuries, Jews continue to re-tell the story of the Passover as though it had just happened to them. How does telling the story as though we were there deepen the meaning of the Exodus? How does it shape our experience with the deliverance that came at Calvary? Even though we have been delivered from sin, we are still on the way to the Promised Land (heaven); how might our story resonate with the forty years of wandering in the desert?

CHAPTER 14

The Old, Old Story of Us and Them

Do you remember that teacher who would read you stories in class, and when the story reached a pivotal moment, she would pull out a bookmark, close the book, and say, "We'll pick up the story again tomorrow and find out what happened to . . ." I'm sure they thought they were being clever—but that's just twisted. What a power trip! But what a truth. Stories grip us and connect us. As a fifth-grader, I started coming to church and Sabbath School, but my fondest memory of those first weeks was the story teacher. I don't remember his name, but he read every week from a book entitled *The Persecutor* by Sergei Kourdakov.[1] His kind voice walked us through the journey of a young Russian secret policeman. The stories of faith, struggle, and discovery were embedded in my heart at the beginning of my personal walk with Christ. The story so influenced my life that later on in my journey, I returned to that book just to recapture the experience of my first steps in faith. Stories capture. Stories teach.

"Love the Lord your God with all your heart, soul and strength." In the previous chapter we were reminded to let these words be on our hearts. But Moses introduced the secret weapon to ensure the flame would pass from one generation to the next. When our children ask, "What does this mean?" instead of offering them simply information, we are to tell them a story—our story of deliverance. Tell anyone who asks how you were a slave in Egypt and how God delivered you with a mighty hand. Tell the story as though you were there. And again, the people that heard these words had never seen Egypt, never experienced crossing the Red Sea—they were born in the desert. Even though they were the second generation, they were commanded to tell the story— that one beautiful story of their redemption—as though they were there.

While the theme of becoming a participant in the narrative of redemption runs throughout Scripture, it does not come easy to us in our culture. In fact, it is a rare feature. But there are still those who can teach us today, in our instant just-add-water society, about entering into the story of the redeemed. Olive Hoehn, a saint in the sunset of her walk home, shares her pilgrimage. We pick up her story as a young adult:

> January of 1941 I went to Portland for my nursing course— too busy for much reading or praying—then married Gus on July 18, 1944 and St. Paul's Hospital for a year of internship and nursery work. Yes, I prayed and studied, but life became so busy—setting up practice and then my family arriving. I'm afraid I still hadn't really learned how to relate to Jesus and God except to keep His commandments and bring my children up like Mother and Dad had brought me up—strict discipline and outward compliance.

> For years I had been trying to gain victory over sin in my life—but I failed repeatedly. I raised my children to be good. It wasn't until about thirty years ago that I really read and understood Ephesians 2:8, 9—"By grace are you saved, through faith, and that not of yourself it is the gift of God. Not of works lest any man should boast." How much plainer could God have said it? All my fighting and determination to do better, and sorrow

for failing so often had nothing to do with my salvation. The battle and fighting had already been done for me by Jesus' temptations in the wilderness and throughout His life on earth and His overcoming and His passion and death on the cross. I had assumed the responsibility of trying to win when He had already won and now He offers me this gift of eternal life, of victory as a "done deal."[2]

We tell our story to declare that we belong, to join the experience of Noah, Abraham and Sarah, Joseph and David and Moses and Esther and Peter—and Olive. As a community of faith, we are disoriented and rudderless if we do not relive the walls of Jericho crumbling or Gideon's army wide-eyed and speechless as God wins the battle. We have no basis— no reference point for mission work—unless we look into the eyes of our Savior who can't stand the thought of losing one of His children to the enemy—so we "go." In a world where a popular phrase warning against meddling in dangerous territory says, "Don't go there," the mantra for believers to "go there" is a must. Today, in our unstoried climate, we have constant news about what is happening immediately around the world, with a continual news ticker at the bottom of the screen displaying scores, weather, and travel information.

And without one story to live by as our reference point, none of this information makes sense or has even a hint of meaning to it. Without that narrative, we struggle to connect personally with our Creator, and we fail to become grateful for our eternal home.

In light of this reality, let me recommend yet another story of the children of Israel. As they stand on the edges of the Promised Land, finally ready to enter in, Captain Joshua speaks to the people. Joshua's speech, in three parts, models the way we participate in the experience of those who are redeemed and find their way home. The first part is about *identifying* with the big story. The second part is Joshua's *inclusion* of their storied journey in the wilderness. And the third part is an *invitation* to enter into the community of believers walking to the Promised Land.

Identifying with their story

Then Joshua assembled all the tribes of Israel at Shechem. He summoned the elders, leaders, judges and officials of Israel, and they presented themselves before God.

Joshua said to all the people, "This is what the LORD, the God of Israel, says: 'Long ago your forefathers, including Terah the father of Abraham and Nahor, lived beyond the River and worshiped other gods. But I took your father Abraham from the land beyond the River and led him throughout Canaan and gave him many descendants. I gave him Isaac, and to Isaac I gave Jacob and Esau. I assigned the hill country of Seir to Esau, but Jacob and his sons went down to Egypt.

" 'Then I sent Moses and Aaron, and I afflicted the Egyptians by what I did there, and I brought you out. When I brought your fathers out of Egypt, you came to the sea, and the Egyptians pursued them with chariots and horsemen as far as the Red Sea. But they cried to the LORD for help, and he put darkness between you and the Egyptians; he brought the sea over them and covered them. You saw with your own eyes what I did to the Egyptians. Then you lived in the desert for a long time' " (Joshua 24:1–7).

Preachers love it when someone, and especially everyone, in the congregation says, "Amen." Not only because it feels good to hears it, but also why it feels good: the congregation identified with something the preacher thought was important. I have watched many student missionaries return from service and share their stories. Without fail, they identify with each other because they were there too. Part of our journey is to learn to identify with the story. The only way to do this is to listen, observe, and try to experience every wonderful detail of the walk home. You weren't there literally, but if your today is going to make sense and if your future has any direction, it is the result of a connection you have to the past. You need to write yourself in as a participant in the story.

This is exactly what Joshua did with Israel. They were not in Egypt; they were now standing on the edge of the Promised Land. It's ironic, but the story of redemption is one story. And even though Joshua and Peter each lived in a particular era, we are all invited to join the unbroken story of going home.

Include your story

Joshua inserts their story at the proper time and place in history.

" 'I brought you to the land of the Amorites who lived east of the Jordan. They fought against you, but I gave them into your hands. I destroyed them from before you, and you took possession of their land. When Balak son of Zippor, the king of Moab, prepared to fight against Israel, he sent for Balaam son of Beor to put a curse on you. But I would not listen to Balaam, so he blessed you again and again, and I delivered you out of his hand.

" 'Then you crossed the Jordan and came to Jericho. The citizens of Jericho fought against you, as did also the Amorites, Perizzites, Canaanites, Hittites, Girgashites, Hivites and Jebusites, but I gave them into your hands. I sent the hornet ahead of you, which drove them out before you—also the two Amorite kings. You did not do it with your own sword and bow. So I gave you a land on which you did not toil and cities you did not build; and you live in them and eat from vineyards and olive groves that you did not plant' " (verses 8–13).

The children of Israel must see their forty-year trek as a part of the grand narrative, so Joshua includes their experience in the walk home. We must do the same. We have the record in Scripture, but our storied life is peppered with pivotal moments. If you try to look at your life as a whole, you will become frustrated. Instead, try to describe your spiritual journey by answering this question: If you had to choose five stories from your life that shaped who you are today, which stories would you choose? They can be stories of victory or defeat—just like Israel's. Some of the most profound experiences of Israel's journey are examples of their lack of faith and vision, as much as any miracle or victory. What events caused you to change, or what changes you sought caused you to have new experiences? How many tries did it take you to finally trust that God would win your battles for you? What was your life like before you experienced God's grace? When were you converted or awakened by God's mercy? What is different about your life now as a result? Be honest and be diligent because stirring up your storied life is not easy.

Without fail I find people who claim, "I don't have a story. I was a raised in a Christian home." You may not identify as much with the children of Israel who suffered in Egypt, but you may identify more with those born in the desert. Peter and Paul would be considered "churched" people who discovered Christ in different ways. We all have a story, and the more we think and work at it, the more our stories come alive and seem to fit. If you don't have time to reflect and try to include yourself in the timeline, what else will you do? Make time. Little by little, work at including yourself in the storied pages of redemption.

It wasn't enough for Joshua and the children of God to identify with those who had gone before. Joshua freezes the crowd and throws down a gauntlet, saying,

> "Now fear the LORD and serve him with all faithfulness. Throw away the gods your forefathers worshiped beyond the River and in Egypt, and serve the LORD. But if serving the LORD

seems undesirable to you, then choose for yourselves this day whom you will serve, whether the gods your forefathers served beyond the River, or the gods of the Amorites, in whose land you are living. But as for me and my household, we will serve the LORD."

Then the people answered, "Far be it from us to forsake the LORD to serve other gods! It was the LORD our God himself who brought us and our fathers up out of Egypt, from that land of slavery, and performed those great signs before our eyes. He protected us on our entire journey and among all the nations through which we traveled. And the LORD drove out before us all the nations, including the Amorites, who lived in the land. We too will serve the LORD, because he is our God" (verses 14–18).

It's not enough to know about the Promised Land. Joshua called people to choose—openly, actively, and deliberately.

Inviting yourself home

Given our history and what we have experienced, what do we choose to do now? Because our journey begs us to focus on our destination as well as to be in touch with our past, we must make a choice—to keep going home. There are trailheads and rabbit runs that detour us away from our heavenly home. Sometimes they seem like God's secret plan for a short-cut, but don't be deceived, it's not the way home. Notice Joshua's words. He doesn't say, "Choose a set of beliefs. Choose a general way of life that leads to heaven. Choose to be on the walk home because it's all about the journey." No, it's not *all* about the journey! It's about Jesus. Joshua says, "Choose this day *whom* you will serve." It's not a point to agree upon; it's a Person to follow.

I would add one final warning. The Israelites responded, "Far be it from us to forsake the LORD to serve other gods!" That's a nice, bold

Peter-like saying you might hear him say in his younger days. But the truth is, forsaking God is not far from us. Serving idols is not *that* far away from our faith in Christ. We learn from Israel's story after they entered the Promised Land that idolatry and forgetting about God and His deliverance is not "far . . . from us."

Peter would say, "Be careful. There is an evil one around you and a sinful nature within you. Be careful to trust fully in God's grace and rest on His promise to deliver and change you. You are holey and you need God's help home. But as you come to understand and trust what God has done for you, bend every effort wholly on practicing God's beautiful virtues. And remember, you are a saint. Don't forget that Calvary made you holy, separate, and set apart for the journey home. And remember that by choosing to walk home to heaven, you choose to enter the storied journey of those who are delivered." Peter's words encourage us: "In keeping with his promise we are looking forward to a new heaven and a new earth, the home of righteousness. So then, dear friends, since you are looking forward to this, make every effort to be found spotless, blameless and at peace with him" (2 Peter 3:13, 14).

We need to start walking home, banking everything on the promise of grace.

We need to stride deliberately as we go and commit to practicing, learning, and experiencing the qualities of God's character. We need to storify how we became people bound for the Promised Land.

Two of my favorite hymns were inspired by a poem written by Arabella Katherine Hankey, a woman who invited herself into the story. During the 1800s, earnest Bible study and spiritual revival stirred England in both the poor and affluent communities. Katherine Hankey was the daughter of a prosperous banker in London who was an integral part of a devoted band of believers who studied, prayed, and used their resources to help others in need. She taught Sunday Schools, became an evangelist, and even worked as a missionary nurse in Africa with her brother. Her life captures the essence of one who seems to "get it." In 1866, she became seriously ill and was bedridden for a year. During that season of sickness, she penned a poem entitled "The Old, Old Story." Part one of the poem was "The Story Wanted"; part two was "The Story Told." From these two poems came the hymns "Tell Me the Old, Old Story" and "I Love to Tell the Story." She recovered from her illness and for many more years walked the storied road home, dying in 1911.

The Old, Old Story

Part I: The Story Wanted

TELL me the old, old Story,
Of unseen things above;—
Of JESUS and His Glory,
Of JESUS and His Love.

Tell me the Story simply,
As to a little child;
For I am weak and weary,
And helpless, and defiled.

Tell me the Story slowly,
That I may take it in—
That wonderful Redemption,
GOD'S REMEDY for sin!

Tell me the Story often,
For I forget so soon!
The "early dew" of morning
Has passed away at noon!

Tell me the Story softly,
With earnest tones and grave;
Remember, I'm the sinner
Whom JESUS came to save.

Tell me the Story always
If you would really be,
In any time of trouble,
A comforter to me.

Tell me the same old Story
When you have cause to fear
That this world's empty glory
Is costing me too dear.

Yes, and when that World's Glory
Shall dawn upon my soul,
Tell me the old, old Story,
"CHRIST JESUS MAKES THEE WHOLE!"

The Old, Old Story

Part II: The Story Told

You ask me for "the Story
Of unseen things above;—
Of JESUS and His Glory,
Of JESUS and His Love."

You want "the old, old Story,"
And nothing else will do!

Indeed I cannot wonder,
It always seems so new!

I often wish that some-one
Would tell it me, each day;
I never should get tired
Of what they had to say.

But I am wasting moments!
Oh! how shall I begin
To tell "the old, old Story,"
How JESUS saves from sin?

Listen, and I will tell you;
God help both you and me,
And make "the old, old Story"
His Message unto thee!

THIS is "THE OLD, OLD STORY";
Say, Do you take it in—
This wonderful Redemption,
GOD'S REMEDY for sin?

Do you at heart believe it?
Do you believe it's true,
And meant for EVERY SINNER,
And, therefore, meant for you?

Then take this "GREAT SALVATION";
For JESUS loves to give!
Believe! and you receive it!
Believe! and you shall live!

And if this simple message
Has now brought peace to you,
Make known "the old, old Story,"
For others need it too.

Let everybody see it,
That Christ has made you free;
And if it sets them longing,
Say, "JESUS died for thee!"

Soon, soon, our eyes shall see Him!
And, in our Home above,
We'll sing "the old, old Story
Of JESUS and His Love!"

I say, "Sing it out!" Right now. Sing as you work, play, or walk. Sing it with your voice, but if your voice is anything like mine, sing it with your life. The more the old story gets connected to your story today, the more walking home makes sense.

---

1. Sergei Kourdakov, *The Persecutor* (New York: Fleming H. Revell, 1974).
2. *The Life and History of Olive Faith Fisher-Hoehn,* a personal family publication.

Questions for Reflection

1. Which stories that you were read or told will you always remember? Why do you think these stories have made such an indelible mark on you?

2. What do you think it means to become a participant or player in the story of redemption?

3. In this chapter, how do we see Joshua identifying with those who left Egypt? What specific words or phrases does Joshua use to insert himself in the metanarrative of salvation?

4. If you were to mark a timeline with the key stories of salvation history and then insert your story between the past and the road yet traveled, how would your story compare to others' stories?

5. Joshua extended the invitation "Who will you serve?" Why do you think Joshua offered the children of Israel the choice? Was this a rhetorical question or a critical part of Israel's journey?

6. What are some deliberate choices you need to make about including yourself in the long line of believers who make their way home?

CHAPTER 15

The Eyes Have It

Read this sentence through once: "Finished files are the result of years of scientific study combined with the experience of many years."

Now read it one more time and count how many times the letter *F* appears in the sentence. There is no trick; just count the *F*s! How many did you find? Most people count three or four. Try it again. There is a total of six, but most people tend to see only three or four. The eyes can be tricked. I don't know why, but many read over and miss exactly what they are looking for. The point is that we need to learn how to see.

John Stilgoe, a distinguished and popular professor at Harvard University, teaches a class on how to see things. Now, if I were to choose a class at Harvard, I would not choose calculus or ancient Greek literature or nuclear physics. I would take Stilgoe's class on the art of exploration. He is the professor of the history of landscape development. We are not talking about spruce trees, grass, or rhododendrons—he teaches students to see things. So, if you were the kind of student who spent all your time staring out the classroom window, then this class is just for you—because looking around is exactly what he teaches. The course description goes a little like this: "I just like to meander along, with or without my students, and just look at everything." The primary objective of the class is to introduce his students to a method of discovering a hidden world that has always been in plain view.

When it comes to walking, the eyes are important. Even people who can see often fail to look at what is front of them. I have maintained for some time now that being blind would be difficult, but more treacherous than blindness is being blind but thinking that you can see just fine. If I know I'm blind, I get help: a cane, a dog, a guide. But even those who start walking with Christ can fail to see what is right in front of them. Leonard Sweet once asked, "How did we get the point but miss the Person?" Peter discovered firsthand the hard truth about learning to see what was right before him at the transfiguration of Jesus.

In Mark 9:2, 3, the journey begins with Jesus, Peter, James, and John walking up a mountain: "Jesus took Peter, James and John with him and led them up a high mountain, where they were all alone. There he was transfigured before them. His clothes became dazzling white, whiter than anyone in the world could bleach them."

The Bible says that Jesus was "transfigured before them." The word *transfigured* describes a change on the outside that results from something on the inside. It is the opposite of *masquerade*, which is an outward change that does not come from within.

As Christ climbs higher, His appearance becomes glorious. But, something happens that initially dims the entire event—the reaction of the disciples to the appearance of Moses and Elijah. The three disciples are in such awe that they are almost speechless in the presence of two visitors from the heaven.

Notice: "And there appeared before them Elijah and Moses, who were talking with Jesus. Peter said to Jesus, 'Rabbi, it is good for us to be here. Let us put up three shelters—one for you, one for Moses and one for Elijah.' (He did not know what to say, they were so frightened.)" (Mark 9:4–6).

Do you know people who simply can't stop talking when they don't know what to say? That's Peter. The brain can't process unless the mouth is moving, which is why some of us should just chew a big wad of gum and save ourselves the embarrassment of having to retract much of what we blurt out. More amazing than Peter being *almost* speechless is the presence of Moses and Elijah. Arguably, Moses and Elijah are the two great prophets in the Old Testament, and Peter is awed by their presence. So, what is so impressive about Moses and Elijah?

Two great prophets

Moses was the lawgiver. Moses received and taught Israel from the days of their bondage to the point where they entered into the Promised Land. Moses was key to their history, their sense of identity. Moses is the one who taught Israel *who* God was and who they were as a people. Peter, James, and John are so enamored with the presence of Moses that the only thing they can say is, "This is good. We should build three tents for you."

But what happens when we become so awestruck by Moses that we fail to see Christ? Consider a familiar story in John 8:3–5.

"The scribes and the Pharisees brought a woman caught in adultery, and having set her in the center of the court, they said to Him, 'Teacher, this woman has been caught in adultery, in the very act. Now in the Law Moses commanded us to stone such women; what then do You say?' " (NASB).

Note this: when you follow Moses instead of the Christ of Moses, it leads you to condemnation. This tendency emerged again in John 9, when the man who Jesus healed of blindness is interrogated by the Pharisees. "Then they asked him, 'What did he do to you? How did he open your eyes?' He answered, 'I have told you already and you did not listen. Why do you want to hear it again? Do you want to become his disciples, too?' Then they hurled insults at him and said, 'You are this fellow's disciple! We are disciples of Moses! We know that God spoke to Moses, but as for this fellow, we don't even know where he comes from' " (John 9:26–29).

It is likely that we all have witnessed the Christless condemnation by people who are sure they are infallibly informed. I'll never forget the time I was a guest speaker on a Christian high school campus, and I decided to join some students on a service project—they were painting an elderly couple's house. After guest teaching a class, I went to my hotel room, put on some blue jeans and a T-shirt, and returned to campus to ride in the van with the students. However, I had to walk through the ad building, and I was unaware there was a dress code—no jeans and no T-shirts. Unfortunately, a teacher saw my attire and grilled me for setting a bad example.

One phrase in her tirade stuck in me: "You need to dress appropriately and remember what this school is all about." I knew what the school was all about because I read their mission statement. I smiled and went into the registrar's office and pulled out the school bulletin, which had the mission statement plastered on the inside front cover. It was a quote from the book *Education,* stating,

> Our ideas of education take too narrow and too low a range. There is need of a broader scope, a higher aim. True education means more than the pursual of a certain course of study. It means more than a preparation for the life that now is. It has to do with the whole being, and with the whole period of existence possible to man. It is the harmonious development of the physical, the mental, and the spiritual powers. It prepares the student for the joy of service in this world, and for the higher joy of wider service in the world to come.[1]

I simply read it aloud to her and asked, "Is that what you were referring to?" I admit that it wasn't the most mature way to respond, but it felt so good—that's another topic. The point is if you see Moses and not the Christ of Moses, it is easy to follow the rules but forget the reason they exist.

Elijah is on the mountaintop as well, and he is a much different kind of prophet from Moses. Elijah is the flamethrower prophet. His contribution is more about the dynamics of a revolution rather than the content of a message. Elijah is sensational, focused on the future, charismatic, and bold. If Moses is about the information, Elijah is about the experience.

But if you focus primarily on Elijah, consider where you might end up. In Luke 9:51–56, Jesus and the disciples are leaving the Samaritan towns having had very little success. The Bible says, "Now it came to pass, when the time had come for Him to be received up, that He steadfastly set His face to go to Jerusalem, and sent messengers before His face. And as they went, they entered a village of the Samaritans, to prepare for Him. But they did not receive Him, because His face was set for the journey to Jerusalem. And when His disciples James and John saw this, they said, 'Lord, do You want us to command fire to come down from heaven and consume them, just as Elijah did?' " (NKJV).

The sons of thunder are so into Elijah. But when you look to Elijah instead of to the Christ of Elijah, it leads to destruction. The lesson is clear: you can draw a line in the sand like that drawn at Mount Carmel and demand that people choose a side, but not every moment is a public showdown between Baal and Jehovah. In fact, Christ would later return to that same region of Samaria and have success, not to mention how the gospel spread in that region after the Resurrection. Jesus reminded the two brothers with barreled-out chests: "Boys, you don't even know what's really going on here—I came to save people, not destroy them" (my paraphrase).

A vision of Moses and not the Christ of Moses leads to condemnation. A focus on Elijah and not the Christ of Elijah can only lead to destruction. Do you ever have such single-minded focus on a good thing that you lose sight of who makes it good?

But notice how God arrests their attention and redirects their focus:

"Then a cloud appeared and enveloped them, and a voice came from the cloud: 'This is my Son, whom I love. Listen to him!' Suddenly, when they looked around, they no longer saw anyone with them except Jesus" (Mark 9:7, 8).

What a beautiful sight that must have been! But it is a sight that had been there all along. Sadly, even after starting the walk home, holey but reborn, we can become single-minded about things that relate to Christ—but miss the Savior altogether.

Max Lucado tells the following parable in the timeless devotional *On the Anvil:*

Once upon a time there was a tiny hamlet in the Swiss Alps. This hamlet was in serious trouble. The well that supplied water to the village went dry. The people began to panic. A river was near the community, but it was located at the bottom of a deep, deep gorge. Hence, no one could reach the water. And it was in the middle of summer, so the snow on the mountain had long since melted.

There was, however, another well flowing with water across the gorge on the adjacent mountainside. An imaginative young thinker came up with a solution. He built a bridge across the gorge.

The villagers were elated.

A bucket brigade was formed immediately, and the water supply was replenished. Needless to say, the bridge became very important to this group. It was their source of life.

They honored the bridge. They named the bridge after the builder and painted it a beautiful gold. Tinsel was strung from the bridge. Miniature bridges were built and sold in the streets. People wore them on their necks and hung them in the windows. A committee was formed to pay homage to the bridge. Only certain people were allowed upon it, and only on certain days, and then only wearing certain clothes. The bridge keeper became the most respected and revered position on the mountain. No one could see or cross the bridge without his permission.

Unfortunately, there were disputes within the committee. The disagreement centered around whether a canopy should be built over the bridge. So the bridge was closed until a decision could be made.[2]

What I love most about the glorious walk home is that it is entirely about Christ. But given our tendencies to become enamored by the peripheral things, I would like to suggest a few trail tips to help us remain focused on Jesus.

Practice starting instead of quitting

People who are able to keep Christ first and foremost are like Paul who says, "Not that I have already obtained it or have already become perfect, but I press on so that I may lay hold of that for which also I was laid hold of by Christ Jesus" (Philippians 3:12, NASB).

The first suggestion is to practice starting instead of quitting. It seems like every call for revival includes a call to quit something instead of a call to start a new way. When our primary emphasis is on what not to do anymore rather than on what to do now, we end up drowning in our own failure. Jesus urged, "Come to Me, all who are weary and heavy-laden, and I will give you rest. Take My yoke upon you and learn from Me, for I am gentle and humble in heart, *and you will find rest for your souls*. For My yoke is easy and My burden is light" (Matthew 11:28–30, NASB; emphasis supplied).

This change in focus can be compared to a driver concentrating on steering rather than on braking. Braking your car slows you and also prevents obvious disasters. But steering guides you to where you want to go. Which is why Calvin Miller states, "Christians are not to be so much quitters as starters. They do not endear themselves to God because of all they lay aside at conversion. Rather, it is what they take up that catches heaven's esteem."[3]

I was studying with a young person who exclaimed with a little frustration: "Just tell me what I'm not supposed to do." And so I handed him a bottle of water and said, "OK, but first tell me what is *not* in this bottled water. Turn it over and look at the ingredients. What is not in water?" He furrowed his brow and stammered, "What do you mean? There is no end to the things I could list that are not in wat—oh." There is an endless list of things not to do, not to watch, not to listen to, not to experience, but there's a simple, short list of things, of ways, to see Christ more fully.

Hosea 6:3 introduces a second suggestion for keeping Christ first and foremost in your life as you walk home. The prophet writes,

"Let us know, let us press on to know the LORD,
　His going forth is as certain as the dawn;
And He will come to us like the rain,
　like the spring rain watering the earth" (NASB).

Practice seeking instead of wondering

The second suggestion is to practice seeking instead of wondering. Some expect God to come to them and pull them in, envelop them, seize them, or possess them. I know sometimes we are taught to ask God to take full control, but I wonder if that is His purpose—to control us. I've never been so possessed by the Spirit that I didn't know what I was doing or what was happening to me. I do know that if all I do is wait for lightning to strike, I'm probably going to miss Him. So, God urges us to seek Him. To search for Him.

Those who wonder and wait for God to show up are like wallflowers at a dance. They are the participants who cling to the chairs against the walls of the room, waiting for someone to pull them in by an invitation to dance. I've been a wallflower Christian. The kind of Christian who is blessed only if something extraordinary occurs—if God doesn't show up in the kind of music I like or the way people around me behave, then I have thought God must not have been in it.

But God Himself said, "If you will seek Me and you will find Me when you seek Me with all your heart" (Jeremiah 29:13). You can get a glimpse of Jesus in the latest Christian book everyone is talking about. You can catch a new angle on the Savior by watching that well-polished video series that portrays Christ in a fresh new way. A lot of people are very passionate about politics and politicians. We all have our favorite authors and artists—we all have mentors and spiritual heroes, but if Christ is to be your focus, then you need to be a seeker instead of a wallflower. He is available throughout the Book. I challenge you to see Him for yourself—firsthand.

- In Genesis, He is the Promised of redemption.
- In Exodus, He is the Deliverer.
- In Leviticus, He is the Lamb.
- In Numbers, He is the Cloud and the Fire.
- In Deuteronomy, He is the Great Rock.
- In Joshua, He is our Captain.
- In Judges, He is the Messenger of Jehovah.
- In Ruth, He is the Kinsman Redeemer.
- In Samuel, He is the prophesied Son of David.
- In Kings and Chronicles, He is the Sovereign One.
- In Ezra, He is the Good Hand of God.
- In Nehemiah, He is the Rebuilder of broken lives.
- In Esther, He is selfless Courage.
- In Job, He is the timeless Creator.
- In Psalms, He is the Good Shepherd.
- In Proverbs, He is the Source of wisdom.

- In Ecclesiastes, He is Truth above the sun.
- In the Song of Solomon, He is the Rose of Sharon.
- In Isaiah, He is Wonderful, Counselor, the Mighty God, the Everlasting Father, He is our Prince of Peace.
- In Jeremiah, He is the Voice of our future.
- In Ezekiel, He is the glorious God.
- In Daniel, He is both the Ancient of Days and the fourth Man in the fiery furnace.
- In Hosea, He is the Faithful Husband.
- In Joel, He is the Spirit's Power.
- In Amos, He is the arms that carry us.
- In Obadiah, He is the God who would humble Edom's pride.
- In Jonah, He is the One who calls us to missions of mercy.
- In Micah, He is the Promise of peace.
- In Nahum, He is our Stronghold.
- In Habakkuk, He pleads for revival.
- In Zephaniah, He is the King who is among us.
- In Haggai, He is the Desire of all nations.
- In Zechariah, He is a cleansing Fountain.
- In Malachi, He is the Sun of Righteousness rising with healing in His wings.
- In Matthew, He is the Messiah.
- In Mark, He is the Suffering Servant.
- In Luke, He is the Son of Man.
- In John, He is the Son of God.
- In Acts, He is the Risen Christ.
- In Romans, He is the Grace of God.
- In Corinthians, He is the greatest Gift of all.
- In Galatians, He is our freedom.
- In Ephesians, He is Head of this church.
- In Philippians, He meets every need.
- In Colossians, He is the preeminent One.

- In Thessalonians, He is the returning Lord.
- In Timothy, He is the faithful Pastor.
- In Titus, He is the Blessed Hope.
- In Philemon, He is the Savior of slaves.
- In Hebrews, He is the Creator, the Perfect Picture of God—the Author of salvation and the Finisher of our faith.
- In James, He is our Judge.
- In Peter, He is the Chief Shepherd.
- In the letters of John, He is the Way, the Truth, the Life.
- In Jude, He is the Archangel Michael.
- In Revelation, He is King of kings and Lord of lords, the Lion of Judah and the Lamb of God, the Alpha and the Omega, and the One who is coming to make all things new.

He is in the very fabric of our makeup as we are created in His image. He is the very center of this Book and the defining moment of history. He is the passion and beauty of the greatest song. And He is available to us today: "This is My Son, listen to Him."

And compared to Christ, no one else is worth our undivided attention. The third suggestion isn't the final one. There are, I'm sure, many more, but it is an important part of staying focused on Christ: practice staying instead of leaving.

Practice staying instead of leaving

Being a Christ-centered person is an enduring experience and not an overnight event. You have to stay long enough for Jesus to make His way through the stuff of our lives. It's like looking at 3-D pictures. I find myself handicapped by my attention span to actually see the image within the image. Clarity comes with time—time to let the dust of our flurried lives settle. Jesus said, "Remain in me, and I will remain in you. For a branch cannot produce fruit if it is severed from the vine, and you cannot be fruitful unless you remain in me" (John 15:4, NLT).

It may be we leave too soon. We are so used to having everything come at us with ever-increasing volume and speed that we have become impatient with the process of discovering Christ. The only way we will know Christ as our primary focus is if we choose to stay until we find Him.

You can see our impatience in everyday conversations with each other. I might say, "Hey, how are you?" And you say, "Fine, how about you?" We may exchange pleasantries, but if we stay long enough, we end up face to face with the awkward moment where we either make up new pleasantries or talk about what is really at the center of our lives. Some avoid those conversations and keep moving. Most of us probably do that with Christ. Instead, we need to stay on our knees or in the pages of Scripture until we see.

The public high school library where I volunteered was closing, and I was on my way out the door when I heard a ruckus. It was a young woman asking for help. I, being a concerned citizen and a devoted eavesdropper, got closer to the action. She was looking through yearbooks, searching for a picture of her biological mother. She held a high school picture of herself and scanned each page of faces to see if she could find the woman who looked like her. What impressed me most was the fight she put up. "I'm not leaving until I find her picture." Two librarians and I helped her look because we knew she meant it. She stayed until she found what she was looking for. The resemblance of that young woman to her mother was simply unmistakable.

Such a single-minded passion for Christ alone is available. Is that what you desire today? On January 12, 2008, a street performer at a subway station in Washington, D.C., began playing his violin just before 8:00 A.M. and played for forty-three minutes. This occurred during the height of morning rush hour. The musician kept his violin case open on the ground near him, just in case anyone wanted to throw a few bucks to the struggling performer.

During that forty-three-minute "concert," 1,097 people passed right by him. Of that number, only seven people stopped and listened for more than a minute or two. At least twenty-seven people made a small contribution to the cause of this penniless violinist. The guy made $32.17 for his early morning concert. How do we know? The event was staged to compile material for an article published in the *Washington Post*. A hidden video camera recorded the entire scene, and researchers were able to analyze and catalogue how many walked by, gave money, or stayed to listen.

So what's the big deal? The violinist was Joshua Bell, one of the greatest classical violinists in the world. Out in the open air, he was playing his Stradivarius worth $3.5 million. That morning, Joshua Bell performed six of the most-acclaimed masterpieces of all time. And only a handful realized it. Commuters were scurrying on their way to work and passed within three feet of this legend. Ironically, people couldn't even get that close to Bell at his sold-out concert at Symphony Hall in Boston just three days prior to his sidewalk performance, where the average ticket price was $100. People didn't even realize what they were missing and who they were not seeing.

- Distracted by the busy life.
- Detoured from the destination home by circumstances and opportunities.
- Derailed from the walk by tragedy or triumph.

Peter begins his last letter by reminding us that it is *His* divine power, *His* gift, *His* promise that ensures our eternal home. We must earnestly see Christ—first and always. If not, we will fail to see where we are going and forget why we started in the first place. Every step toward home is taken with a clear sense that I am not right, good, or full without the mercy of Christ. That realization keeps the basis of our walk firmly on Jesus. Will there ever be a point in our lives on this earth, or in our home

214 • LIVE Like You *Mean It*

to come, where we will become so good we forget why there are scars in Jesus' hands? If we are going to be enamored by His sacrifice throughout eternity, we will also be mindful of how broken we are without Him. I can live with that.

---

1. Ellen G. White, *Education* (Nampa, Idaho: Pacific Press® Publishing Association, 1952), 13.

2. Max Lucado, *On the Anvil* (Carol Stream, Ill.: Tyndale, 1994).

3. Calvin Miller, *Into the Depths of God* (Grand Rapids, Mich.: Bethany House, 2001).

Questions for Reflection

1. When you answered the question in the opening paragraph, did you see all the *F*s? Why do you think most people miss some of them? Typically, older people tend to read past some of the *F*s more than younger people do. Why do you think that might be?

2. Do you agree or disagree with the statement that "more dangerous than being blind is being blind but thinking you can see just fine." Explain.

3. Leonard Sweet asks the question, "How did we get the point but miss the Person?" What does he mean by this question? When in your life have you missed the Person?

4. Why do you think the Transfiguration story is included in the Bible? What salient truths does it convey?

5. Is there a tendency for people to follow a modern-day Moses or Elijah instead of Christ? What message does God have for you in this story?

6. What might happen to Christians' mind-sets if we shifted our focus from what we give up to what we take on when we start the journey home?

7. As you review the way Christ is central to all the books of the Bible, which book surprised you? Which book intrigued you? In which book of the Bible have you found Christ to be unmistakably present and real?

8. What does staying look like for you in a world that is so pressured to move along? What do you think it means to stay until Christ becomes clear?

9. How does telling the story of our redemption, the biblical story and our present story, keep our steps pointed toward home?

CONCLUSION

That's My Story and I'm Sticking to It

One of my students wrote, "Whenever you have a task to do or a decision to make, ask, 'What would Jesus do?' " Wouldn't it simplify all our choices if we aligned them against this principle? What would it look like?

I watched a young boy not more than nine arguing with a young girl about the same age as they played together in the yard. The conflict boiled to a head, and what happened next, if taken literally, was biblical. It was clear that the girl was not seeing things the same way as the boy was. In fact, he believed not only that she couldn't see things his way, but that she couldn't see at all—she must have been blind. So it begs the question, What would Jesus do with someone who was obviously suffering from blindness? According to John 9, Jesus placed mud on a blind man's eyes and told him to go wash it out. The young boy answered the challenge to mirror the actions of the Savior and unceremoniously threw mud in the eyes of his little friend. Just ask, "What would Jesus *do?*" Right?

I had a student who obeyed this rule of life without failure. Whenever we had company and cars were parked out front, demonstrating a party or a dinner was in progress, he would simply ask, "What would Jesus do?" Scripture clearly states that Jesus ate and drank with sinners—and those gathered at my house, especially me, clearly fit that description.

After all, only a sinner would fail to invite Michael to the dinner. He even followed the WWJD challenge by confronting us in the same manner that Christ came to Zacchaeus and would say, "I'm coming to your house today!" Now that is what Jesus would do!

And so, recently, I received a lovely gift of a large box of Ghirardelli various dark chocolates. And returning to my house, I saw several cars camped outside our drive and across the street. Several students lounged in the front yard with plates of food. Another gathering—probably the result of one of Michael's initiatives, and I, too, seized by conviction asked the question, What would Jesus do? Now on one occasion in Matthew 9, it says that when Jesus saw the crowds He had compassion on them, but that wasn't the example that came to mind. I looked at the ample box of chocolates and I looked at the crowd at my house and asked, What would Jesus do? In gospel of Mark, Jesus, when pressed by the crowd, would go to a solitary place—WWJD. Just me and my chocolate!

What would Jesus do? The phenomenon resurged a few years ago when a youth group in Michigan read Charles Sheldon's classic, *In His Steps,* in which individual Christians in a town began trying to live by a simple rule—to whatever scenario in their lives, they would ask, What would Jesus do? In his simple style, Sheldon tells the story of self-satisfied congregants of a midwestern church who are challenged by a tramp during a Sunday service to live up to their declaration of faith. The tramp then dies in their midst. So moved are the minister and his parishioners that they pledge to live their lives for one year asking themselves, What would Jesus do? Their example, how they suffered, faced ridicule, and emerged victorious inspired other churches throughout the country to do the same.

And although the slogan has become a bit of a marketing fad, think about what would happen if people tried to follow in the steps of Jesus? There is value in thinking about how to orient life so that one is guided by a principle.